Increasingly, we are aware of the pain, sorrow, and confusion that follow in the wake of a divorce, which, unfortunately, has become disastrously commonplace in our culture. Not the least of those who suffer are the children. Lynn Cassella has written a thoughtful and practical book to help young people work their way through the great disruption that follows divorce. With a compassion borne of her own experience, she helps the reader see that others have gone through heartaches that often seem impossible both to comprehend and absorb. She aids by addressing the disaster of divorce with intellectual honesty, leading the reader to appropriate once again the value and need for forgiveness, the importance of getting possession of one's life again, and the realization that even so great a trial as this is but one cross that a Christian, by prayer, openness to God's grace, and perseverance, can endure.

+ Most Reverend Donald W. Wuerl
Bishop of Pittsburgh

Finally, a very practical tool for adolescents and young adults of divorce. This will assist them in finding peace and closure to their experience. Lynn's sensitivity comes from both personal experience and exceptionally well-developed insight. Clinicians will find it a useful tool in working with this population.

Dr. Patricia Henel
Family Therapist

Lynn's story reveals the painful aftermath of her parents' divorce, but more importantly it reveals the empowering qualities of forgiveness and faith. This book has helped me to understand that working through my own feelings of denial, anger, and grief is well worth the effort.

Lauren Cutuly
Age 22

Lynn Cassella provides a valuable and usable resource for the pastoral care of young people. Many youth experience the difficulties and struggles related to divorce and this book provides insight and fosters healing. Useful for individual reflection by young people, small group sessions, and as a resource for parents, catechists, teachers, and youth ministers, "Making Your Way" describes the spectrum of emotional and relational issues and includes reflection and journal questions and exercises. I especially appreciate the attention to the faith dimension and one's relationship with God in the experience of divorce, as well as the clear and concise presentation of Church teachings on marriage, divorce, and annulment.

Bob McCarty, D.min.
Executive Director
National Federation for Catholic Youth Ministry

As a psychology student, it is easy for me to see that any divorce will affect a child's behaviors, feelings, and motivations. As a child of divorced parents, it is much harder for me to determine the source of my own emotions and actions.

Lynn's book provided a source of understanding and comfort during a time that is filled with confusion and anxiety. She challenged me to get to the heart of how divorce impacted the dynamics of my family and myself. Simple to read, yet powerful in its implications, Lynn's book is a guide for any child seeking to understand the division they never deserved.

Elissa Cutuly
Age 20

A beautiful, sensitive and practical guide for any family facing the adjustments of divorce. A must read for teenagers and young adults of divorced parents. It brings God's peace and healing to the human heart!

Carol Tempel
Coordinator, Family Life Ministry
Archdiocese of St. Louis

I have been in much the same situation as Lynn, and this book has been an eye opener for me. Lynn Cassella shows that being a child of divorce brings many different feelings and emotions. What is important for us is to accept the divorce as being beyond our control. After one is able to forgive and accept the given situation, we can become stronger persons for ourselves and for our family.

Heather Balest
Age 25

Lynn Cassella has done "a divorced generation" a marvelous service. By sharing her story, she will make numerous young (and not so young) people take a good look at who they are and what they can grow into. She reveals a life journey where walking with God in faith can take us to Catholic and Christian maturity. Our past does not have to limit us—it can propel us into becoming whole, holy, and responsible beings.

Lynn's step-by-step approach will inspire so many to have the courage to take ownership with their lives. A.A. has its twelve steps; now the children of divorce have thirteen chapters to walk to a new freedom.

I wish I would have had this resource years ago.

The Rev. John Dennehy
Newark Newman Center

Coping with the divorce of one's parents is a daunting challenge for any young man or woman. In this book, Lynn Cassella provides a structured, step-by-step process to begin to understand, digest, and then move past the whirlwind of emotions that a child of divorce is confronted with. I have found this book an enriching and ameliorating experience and sincerely hope that this "healing tool" will reach many of the young people who are in desperate need of the type of understanding, empathy, and emotional empowerment that this work provides.

Michael Caprino
Age 25

Making Your Way

after your parents' divorce

a supportive guide
for personal growth

Lynn
Cassella

**Foreword by
Father Theodore
Hesburgh, C.S.C.**

ONE LIGUORI DRIVE, LIGUORI, MO, 63057-9999

Imprimi Potest:
Richard Thibodeau, C.Ss.R.
Provincial, Denver Province
The Redemptorists

Imprimatur:
Most Reverend Timothy M. Dolan
Auxiliary Bishop, Archdiocese of Saint Louis

ISBN 0-7648-0872-9
Library of Congress Catalog Number: 2002100277

© 2002, Lynn Cassella
Printed in the United States of America
02 03 04 05 06 5 4 3 2 1

Liguori Lifespan is an imprint of Liguori Publications.

Scripture quotations are from the *New Revised Standard Version of the Bible*, copyright © 1989 by the Division of Christian Education of the National Council of Churches of Christ in the USA. Used with permission. All rights reserved.

Excerpts from the English translation of the *Catechism of the Catholic Church* for use in the United States of America copyright © 1994, United States Catholic Conference, Inc.—Libreria Editrice Vaticana. English translation of the *Catechism of the Catholic Church: Modifications from the Editio Typica* copyright © 1997, United States Catholic Conference, Inc.—Libreria Editrice Vaticana. Used with permission.

This book is not intended to replace the advice of psychologists or other healthcare professionals. It should be considered an additional resource only. Questions and concerns about mental health should always be discussed with a healthcare provider.

To order, call 1-800-325-9521
www.liguori.org
www.catholicbooksonline.com

Contents

With love, I dedicate this book to my parents who instilled my faith in God and to my husband who nurtures that faith by his love and example each day.

Acknowledgments

I am profoundly grateful to all the teens, young adults, and families whom I have learned from over the years. This includes, in particular, my own family with whom I have learned the most and who have provided me with individual examples of courage.

With deep love and appreciation, I especially thank my husband, George Kapusinski, who believed in me and supported me continually as I wrote. Through his example of faith and positive spirit, he served as my greatest inspiration.

I am indebted to my editor, Hans Christoffersen, who provided his talent for conciseness, clarity, and command of language, and who never failed to encourage me with kindness and enthusiasm. I am also fortunate to have had the leadership of Elsie McGrath, who was gracious to me as a writer and receptive to the idea for this book. In addition, I thank my endorsers for their thoughtful review and for sharing important insights for all readers.

Finally, I give special thanks to the Reverend Theodore M. Hesburgh, C.S.C., for offering generous support and leadership through his foreword and for exemplifying to me what it means to serve God.

The names in this book have been changed and the identities of the persons whose stories are told have been disguised in order to protect the confidentiality and sacredness of friendship and of the ministerial relationship.

Foreword

This is an ambitious and courageous undertaking, and one that Lynn Cassella has pursued with love for you, her brothers and sisters of divorce. It is her effort to pull together the most meaningful aspects of her personal journey and share them in a compassionate, challenging, and insightful way. She has done this because she very much wants to make your path less difficult and help you grow. And because she believes in your ability to make this struggle work for you.

You are in the hands of an authority. Lynn not only has studied Catholic teachings but she has also triumphed over the struggles you're experiencing, relying on her faith and Jesus' example. She shows in this book an ability both to empathize and guide, to "talk the talk and walk the walk." Rather than avoiding suffering, she becomes intimate with it. She is acutely attentive, also, to the range of your feelings, largely, in my estimation, because of what her own experience has taught her.

Today, we are living in a culture in which the sanctity of marriage is often disregarded, encouraging persons to enter into this commitment without the necessary mental, emotional, and spiritual readiness. This has encouraged the present crisis of divorce and, consequently, the crisis of children of divorce. If we want to safeguard the prosperity of our nation, we all need to heighten our consciousness, not just of the problem, but of what we can do to help eradicate it.

This prosperity depends upon emotional healthiness which, I believe, is achieved by seeing our struggles through the eyes of faith. Jesus' statement holds true just as much today as it did over two thousand years ago: "Take my yoke upon you and learn from me, for I am meek and humble of heart; and you will find rest for yourselves" (Matthew 11:29). I translate this to mean that it is only by embracing the pain and trials of our lives that we unite ourselves with Jesus, and thereby reap the benefits of God's grace and direction in overcoming struggles.

Certain events in my own life have led me toward faith and religion as the only answer for truly rising above difficulties. Today, I am convinced that both hold the solutions to the most important problems of human life and to personal suffering in particular.

It is this solution that this book also upholds. In it, you will meet a woman whose devotion to God has made a difference in her life, who has learned through prayer, Jesus' example, and following the dictates of her heart to let God guide her life, and thereby share her wisdom with you. In so doing, she invites you to open your heart to this same reality of Jesus walking with you. I highly recommend this book to both practicing and nonpracticing Christians, believers and nonbelievers, as well as lay and professional persons. It offers not a treatise on faith or religion, but an example of what both are meant to do.

FR. THEODORE M. HESBURGH, C.S.C.
PRESIDENT EMERITUS, UNIVERSITY OF NOTRE DAME

Introduction

I have written this book because I know from personal experience how difficult it can be to resolve the problems and hurt caused by our parents' divorce. It took me a long time to do so, and during much of that time I had little outlet for my feelings and little knowledge regarding what goal and "tools" would best resolve them. At times, I intuitively did the "right thing" but, just as often, I held on to false beliefs and claimed too much responsibility and other reactions that only served to keep me "stuck."

In this book, I give you the best of what I've learned, both what helped me grow and heal as well as what was in my way. The circumstances surrounding my parents' divorce will likely differ from yours. However, through my sharing and you reflecting on your own journey, you'll see that we share similar grief and, together, can find a path to wholeness.

Another major motivation for writing this book is the amount of negative messages often touted about young people of divorce. These broad generalizations are often misleading and negative, and can lead us to expect only personal failure. Worse, these negative stereotypes may influence us to adopt the identity of "powerless victims" who either use our parents' divorce as an excuse for not doing better or deny that the divorce has any impact on who we are.

This book can be used in a variety of ways:

1. **If you are a high school or college student:**
   a. Use it on your own.
   b. Share it in a one-on-one setting with your best friend, counselor, church leader, or anyone else you trust.
   c. Use it to start a discussion group in your school or church.
2. **If you are a religious educator, youth minister, social worker, or psychologist:**
   Use the questions in this book to establish a support group. The text will help you better understand the difficulties of divorce from a young person's perspective and what insights will help them heal.
3. **If you are a divorced parent:**
   Use it as a road map to follow in discussions with your children. Instead of telling them how they ought to feel or behave, this book provides the questions that will help them think for themselves and thereby more fully express and resolve their grief.

As you read this book, you will find yourself on a special journey of healing. At times, you may discover insights that offer you greater perspective and thereby peace. At other times, you may find it scary and painful to dig into the feelings the questions evoke. One thing you can be assured of: what you get from this journey will depend on how much you invest in it. If you stay with it, you will find that these challenges have the potential to benefit you more than any others in this area of your life.

Each chapter begins with a vignette that highlights an emotion or difficulty often experienced as a result of our parents' divorce. Use them as mirrors for looking at your own life. Throughout each chapter, you will also find reflection and journal questions and exercises to help you take a deeper look at your own situation. As you work through your feelings and consider better ways to resolve your problems, you will begin to learn more about yourself and see your struggles in a new light.

You will need a notebook or a legal pad when answering the reflection and journal questions. Use this space as your own private place to write in as much and as often as you'd like. While writing, you might also discover questions of your own that you'd like to ask in your discussion group or with someone you trust.

You will also be encouraged to reflect on your relationship with God and view your struggles through the eyes of faith. In looking back on my journey, I do not think it would have been possible for me to have risen above my grief without drawing on the help of the Lord without whom these difficulties are too great and too heavy for the human heart to handle.

The challenge of making your way after your parents' divorce presents you with two options: you can either ignore or fight the pain and let it consume you more as a result; or you can choose to enter it, much like Jesus did at his passion, work your way through it with God's help, and experience a whole new sense of freedom and joy. The goal of this book is to help you with the latter as you take ownership of your feelings, examine your struggles, and search for your own answers about relationships, God, and faith. Running away from the challenge will only encourage you to carry unresolved hurts into your relationships and either burden them with unrealistic expectations or shortchange them by "playing it safe."

My prayer for you is that you find the strength and courage to let yourself "be broken" instead of fighting your brokenness. Facing your parents' divorce is facing a loss, one that no one or nothing can replace. Just like the acceptance of other losses, you'll need to grieve your pain in order for healing to begin. Let yourself "break" and ask God for strength. Little by little, you will find yourself moving past it. It happened to me, and it can happen to you, too.

CHAPTER ONE

Denial

The priest lifts a round, softball-sized, white wafer above the altar. He holds it in front of him, staring at it. A bright light shines down on his face. I think of God looking at him from above. The priest puts down the wafer, then kneels slowly, keeping the palms of his hands fixed on top of the altar. It's Lent, the time when Dad left last year.

The priest cups his hands around the chalice and continues to pray. I know God wouldn't let Dad be so important to me only to take him away for good. God wants me to keep loving Dad, and that means I have to keep waiting. God wants me to keep believing Dad's coming back and have hope, so that's what I'm going to do. The priest kneels slowly one more time.

The ushers start down the aisle. I get up from the pew and take my place at the end of the line. I stand there and think about Dad, wondering what he's doing. I figure he must be going to communion too because, as I step closer to the altar, I feel like he's right there with me, and that it's only a matter of time before he comes back for real.

For a long time after my dad left home, I refused to see anything about him and his love for me as different from what I wanted to see. At eleven years of age, I couldn't even acknowledge how much both our lives had changed. I refused to let anything or anyone upset my picture-perfect world.

1

My father moved ever farther away from us and our family. I was a high school senior when I finally accepted the fact that he wasn't coming back to be the father I had always thought he'd be. An avalanche of questions and negative feelings consumed me: How could he not call, write, or see me more often? Did he think about me at all anymore? If he really loved me, why did he move so far away? I was haunted and felt so unsure of myself. It was as if I couldn't go out in the world and make something of myself until I had a handle on who my father really was and the nature of his love for me.

Getting answers was especially difficult for me, however. By this time, my father was living clear across the country, which made our visits infrequent and brief. On occasion, I tried to get details from my mom, but she was understandably still upset and unable to discuss the matter with much objectivity. I had to come up with my own answers, but many of them were often incorrect because they were based on too little information.

- What pressing questions do you have regarding your parents' divorce and/or your relationships with them now?
- What "information" do you need to know that would help you make better sense of it all?
- What have you done to get the information you need?
- Have you been successful? If not, what could you do or whom could you talk with to get the right answers?

Sometimes, I thought the worst of my dad, but more often I rationalized or made excuses for what I didn't understand or what was difficult to accept about him. Just as in the vignette when I was a girl, so too as a teenager, I wasn't willing to see any unpleasant realities. Oftentimes, my denial showed itself as shame. I blamed myself for my father's lack of involvement in my life, telling myself I wasn't getting more attention because I didn't really deserve it. "I haven't achieved anything really great," I'd think, "so why should Dad take more of an interest in me?" The bottom line: It was all "my fault" or "my mistake."

Seeing our parents' limitations and weaknesses is difficult because it means seeing the ways in which they *can't* meet our needs or be there for us.

- What are the good beliefs you are clinging to about your parents, beliefs that have shown themselves to be either false or likely false?
- What present realities contradict those beliefs?
- Are you rationalizing or making excuses for the behavior of your parent(s) because it's easier than admitting that this behavior is wrong or careless? If so, what behaviors are difficult for you to acknowledge?
- What shortcomings do your parents have that hinder or prevent them from meeting your needs?
- What traits in your parents are most difficult for you to accept?

I bought into denial and shame so much that it took over my life. One example involved my schoolwork. I centered my life around achieving straight A's. However, I soon found that making high honor roll and getting awards in school didn't earn me more attention and approval from my father. I gave into more denial and set even higher criteria for myself: "When I graduate from medical or law school...when I have a thriving practice or win my first big case...when my accomplishments get written about in the newspaper...." I continued to push away reality, denying my loss, and rejecting real responsibility for my future.

- How has denial affected your life?
- How is it affecting it now?
- Has it affected your life in seemingly positive ways? If so, how?
- Do you tolerate and/or make excuses for shoddy treatment from your friends?
- Do you sometimes feel like you're not good enough to be treated better?

My denial would, at times, lead me to make secret bargains with God. I knew it was good to have God on my side; however, as in the vignette, instead of making a general call for help, I approached God as a sort of Santa Claus who existed to grant my requests, especially when I did something pleasing, like going to communion. I failed to realize that I was clinging to a wish and not a hope.[1]

- Have you made or are you making bargains with God? If so, what are they?
- What are you trying to prevent yourself from accepting? What do you really need help with instead?

It took a lot of courage, as well as humility, for me to move past denial. I didn't want to face the losses of my situation, and I didn't want to face the responsibilities that were placed on my shoulders as a result. I wanted to make something good of myself, and I needed my dad's help to get there. And while he did help me, it wasn't in the ways I needed most. It was difficult for me to see and accept this fact, because it meant I was alone and solely responsible for getting to where I wanted to go.

I also had to learn to adopt a constructive attitude toward my situation and find ways to befriend this rejected part of myself. You might be wondering how it's possible to do this. Like looking at a blemish smack-dab on the front of your nose and feeling good about it, how can you regard this aspect of your life in a positive way? It starts by being open to and looking for the deeper good contained in it. My parents' divorce definitely helped me grow in terms of compassion, empathy, and understanding. It also strengthened my resolve to "get marriage right," along with my relationship with God.

- What stands most in your way of confronting the reality of your situation (e.g., fear of grief, embarrassment, lack of confidence in standing alone, lack of support)?
- What are some of the benefits that may result from owning your negative feelings and struggle?
- What opportunities for growth does it give you that others without this problem lack?

---

[1] In Chapter Four, "Grief," I explore wishes and hopes more fully.

- Is it difficult for you to accept that the world isn't always fair?
- How might your view of the world encourage your denial?

While denial may serve as a short-term buffer for pain or as a reprieve when we're overwhelmed, it never helps in resolving our problems. Instead, it leads to bigger obstacles down the road because it encourages us to avoid personal responsibility for our own happiness and thereby our emotional maturity.

A denial in one area often leads to a denial in another, and so on. In my case, I didn't even realize the extent of my denial until I encountered problems in my first serious dating relationship after college. I overreacted so much in that relationship that it showed me the extent of my unresolved feelings toward my father.[2]

- Has your boy/girlfriend or another close friend ever told you that you were overreacting to something they said or did?
- If so, what specifically caused you to overreact?
- Consider these situations more objectively. Might there be a past hurt lurking in the background that you've been denying?
- What hurt might be triggering your overreaction?

Our rocks of pain can eventually turn to diamonds of peace; however, we need to let God help us. We need the courage to confront our loss and the patience to "let go and let God," as difficult as that can be at times. We all want life to be fair, and most of us want to control what happens to us. However, just as I had to learn as a young girl, God doesn't promise us a problem-free "perfect world." Instead, what we are offered is divine strength to move through and rise above it. Seeing and approaching difficulties through the eyes of faith enables us to live the deeper meaning and purpose contained in them. Not only do we grow more fully, we appreciate life more deeply.

---

[2] In Chapter Eight, "Dating Relationships," I explore this issue in detail.

Notes

CHAPTER TWO

Shame

Jared takes his time untangling the rope in the water. His body rocks back and forth with the waves. It's the last time he'll be going waterskiing for the summer; he's leaving for college on Monday. If only he could take a year off and help Mr. Peterson with his lake resort business. That would be the ideal job, working with people he's known most of his life. Instead, he has to meet a bunch of strangers. Most of them are probably phony liars just like his dad.

He flings the rope in between his skis and curls his body into a ball. What a spineless thing his dad did, lying to everyone about being on Prozac™. Flat-out denied it, right to Jared's face, when he found the pill bottle. No way he'll believe anything his dad tells him now.

Jared flashes two fingers, then seven at the driver, the same speed he always chooses. He straightens his arms and bends his knees. The boat yanks him out of the water. He looks at the mountains on both sides of him and smiles. He likes this view of the lake best.

One of the guys in the boat chugs down some beer. Jared remembers how his dad drank the entire weekend Jared last visited him. He shouldn't drink like that when taking medicine. What a reckless thing to do. Would he become an alcoholic like Grandpa? Maybe Jared was doomed to become an alcoholic too.

He clasps the handle tighter, leans right, pointing his skis straight at the wake. He blasts over it. His skis dip down. Then, Jared speeds away from the boat. After a few seconds, his body starts bouncing all over from the choppy water. He bends his knees more. He sure isn't going to invite any of his buddies to his dad's house anymore.

He leans left and skis back behind the boat. His grandfather's example should motivate his dad to do better. His dad must not think Jared's worth it. He watches the calm water in front of him. He likes how it never changes and makes a clear path for him. He wishes he could count on his dad to tell him the truth, no matter what it was. Then he probably wouldn't feel so unimportant, like a loser, all the time.

The boat heads toward Jared's favorite spot on the lake, a bay with huge trees and rocks. He doesn't feel like skiing anymore, though. He lets go of the handle and sinks slowly into the water.

Even though I knew my parents' divorce was their mistake, it seemed as if I'd never be able to shake the dark cloud that hung over my head because of it. Whether it was going to Mass on Sunday morning with my mom and seeing the church filled with fathers or sitting alone in my dorm room not knowing whom to talk to about my major, I consistently felt like "damaged goods," "discarded" and as if I'd never be "good enough" because my father wasn't more involved in my life. I knew I had talents and enough intelligence, but I needed my father's approval of who I was and wanted to be before I felt I would "measure up."

- What do your parents do (or not do) that causes you to feel as though you're "not good enough"?
- What negative feelings has this caused you to have about yourself? Journal your answer.
- Write down the "you" statements you hear "inside" (e.g., "You'll never be able to attain your goals, because you're not good enough.").
- Who or what causes these feelings? (Maybe someone in your family actually said these "you" statements.)
- Rewrite these "you" statements as positive "I" statements (e.g., "I am hard-working and intelligent and get work done ahead of time.").

My dad wasn't like the "deadbeat dads" whose whereabouts are unknown and whom lawyers have to chase down for money. I was fortunate in that my dad always provided for me financially and wrote to me often during the years right after he left home. He was open about his feelings too, openly admitting his guilt and shame regarding the divorce. However, I still remained a girl who longed for her father's affirmation and approval more than anything. That approval was not forthcoming, and I accepted the self-defeating messages that came my way because of it: "You're pretty worthless. Your father must not think very much of you. You're a reject." I lived in that dark place that told me I was "insignificant" and "did not exist." I clung to shame.

> Shame is a dangerous emotion because it causes us to disown ourselves.

I didn't even want to think about who I was because I was convinced I wouldn't like what I'd see. I couldn't shake the obvious fact that hit me each day: My dad was not involved in my life. He did not "claim" me as his daughter. I couldn't help but feel there was something really wrong with me because of it. I buried my needs in shame.

Our parents can encourage our shame in direct ways as well. For instance, I've heard divorced parents vent their unresolved anger at their former spouse toward their children, saying things like "You're just like your father" or "Your dad used to do the same thing." Statements like these often serve only to increase our shame when the "ex-parent" has set a bad example for us. When our same-sexed parent is responsible for the behavior, it becomes that much easier to view it as a negative reflection on ourselves.

- Does anyone in your inner circle of family and friends give you direct, negative messages about yourself? If so, who?
- Might their message speak to a problem within themselves instead of one within you? If so, what problem might they be experiencing?
- Is your shame a response to your mother's and/or father's desertion or abandonment of you?
- If so, instead of assuming responsibility for this action, what other reason(s) might be a better explanation for their actions?
- Are your parents feeling shame because of the divorce? If

so, what have they done or said that reveals it? Has their shame increased yours?
- What choices do you make regularly that encourage your feelings of worthlessness and shame?

Your parents' actions or lifestyle might also be shaming you indirectly. Jared certainly took personally his father's lie and failure to curb his drinking problem. Consider how Jared took it to mean that his dad didn't love him, that Jared was a "loser," and that he could easily become an alcoholic himself.

Shame led me to feel like I was always on the outside looking in, observing rather than participating in life. I felt alienated and isolated from the world, just as I did from my father. This led to feelings of powerlessness and defenselessness.

I saw my mother as "left behind," like I was, and this doubled my shame. I clung to incorrect attitudes about responsibility as a result, instead of wrestling with the harder questions it posed.

- What decisions do you have to make that your shame is causing you to ignore?
- In what areas do you need to take more responsibility for the quality of your life?
- Do you feel powerless, defenseless, or unprotected because of your parents' divorce? If so, in what way(s)?
- What groups in your school or community might lend you the support you need (e.g., clubs, sports teams, church youth groups, etc.)?
- What friendships are good for you, allowing you to feel accepted and loved for who you are?

Luckily, my shame didn't lure me into crime, drugs, promiscuity, or the like, but it did require me to cover up just the same. That cover-up consisted in achieving good grades, awards, and leadership positions in school. The affirmation I received from these pursuits enabled me to feel, "Yes, I am good enough." However, the feeling never lasted long since I didn't believe it.

These cover-ups never break shame's vicious circle because they persuade us to base our self-worth on the values of the outside world rather than on our own intrinsic goodness. If we define ourselves by the world's values, we will always come up short and never find last-ing satisfaction and fulfillment.

> In order to reduce shame, we need to remind ourselves, over and over, of all that is good about who we are.

Jared forgot to recall his strong points. When Jared started feeling shameful, he needed to consider the facts that contradicted the nega-tive messages which came his way—he needed to cling to self-love, not self-defeat.

- What are all the good aspects about who you are?
- In what ways do you try to cover up your shame?

In addition to my dad, I based my self-worth on the opinions and treatment I received from male teachers, male bosses, and sometimes even the men I dated. I exerted tremendous effort to win affirmation from them, whether by getting the best grade, spending extra hours to polish work projects and refer clients, or by trying to impress a date in some way. I never received enough approval, however, nor did I end up giving my dating relationships the chance to grow.

- Are you looking to any person to give you a sense of self worth? If so, who and in what way(s)?
- Are these relationships growing or not? What effect has your lack of self-love had on these relationships?
- In what small and big ways could you work on nurturing self-love?
- Do you ever feel precious? How could you make these ex-periences a bigger part of your life?

Not only did nurturing self-love offer me contentment, it also gave way for the Holy Spirit to enter my life and guide me. Through hobbies like reading, for example, I developed a great love for writing that led me to apply to graduate school and finally discover the ca-reer path that was right for me. Little by little, I bought into positive messages about who I was and my abilities. I began to give myself an honest chance while cultivating a life based on my values and de-sires. By listening to these positive messages, I found myself gaining ever more courage to take the risks that were necessary to get what I wanted. This newfound strength was born out of my growing relationship with God and the space I made for the Spirit to guide me. The more I opened myself to God, the more I was led and, with each step, I discovered greater self-love because I was discovering God's love for me in a profound way.

- In what ways do your career aspirations, friends, dating relationships, and hobbies reflect who you are as well as your values and desires?
- What aspects of your life do not reflect these values and desires?
- Do you believe that God loves you, despite your weaknesses?
- What leads you to believe or not believe in God's love?
- What persons and/or opportunities have entered your life that might demonstrate God's love for you?

Learning to love myself was a crucial step in my healing. It gave me the strength and insight to view my parents' divorce in a different way as well. Instead of regarding it as a "mark" against me, I looked for the positive opportunities in it. I set out to learn and grow in understanding, compassion, and conviction. This attitude enabled me not only to reap good from the bad, but also to see this difficulty as essential to my discovering and fulfilling God's plan for my life.

CHAPTER THREE

Guilt

That casserole was really good, Mom," Sarah says. She and her mother have just finished dinner. Sarah picks up the dirty dishes and sets them beside the sink. She notices the Legal Association cookbook on the counter and points to it. "Did you get the recipe in there?"

"No, Aunt Betsy gave it to me." Her mom looks back at her hardback novel.

Sarah watches her mom's face to determine if it's a good time or not to mention her conversation with her dad.

"I don't see any of *your* recipes in here." Sarah reads out loud some of the titles along with the women who submitted them. Her mom continues reading.

"Weren't you involved with this group?" Sarah waits for a response, hoping the subject might get her mom to mention her dad first.

Her mom sets down the book. "No, your father wouldn't let me do anything when you were young. I even had to wait until you were asleep before I could do the laundry. He said I should be right there with you at all times no matter what you were doing. Your plate always had to have all kinds of different colored vegetables on it. He insisted on it, said it was necessary so you'd eat well."

Sarah leans back against the counter, thinking: "Dad was really that protective of me?"

Her mom looks back at her novel. She turns a page. Sarah doesn't know if her mom's disappointment has to do with her dad, her, or both of them. There will probably never be a good time to mention her plans.

Sarah clears her voice. "Mom, there's something I want to tell you." Her heart is beating so hard and fast, it feels like it's about to explode right through her chest.

Her mother looks her straight in the eye.

Sarah folds her arms and grabs hold of her elbows. "You know, I really appreciate all the clothes you bought me and everything you're doing to help me get ready for college. You've gone to a lot of trouble." She holds her elbows tighter. Her mom continues to look at her. Sarah hates being put in this situation. Her mom is going to feel left out, and there's nothing Sarah can do about it. The last thing she wants is to do something that hurts her mom. Maybe it was selfish for her to have accepted her dad's offer.

"So, what's on your mind?"

"Dad wants to drive me to school and stay for orientation."

Her mother snaps the book shut. "I thought you wanted *me* to see the campus and meet your roommates."

"I do. I still want you to come for Parents' Weekend. It's just that Dad already rented a *U-haul™* and said he'd get me whatever extra furniture I need."

Her mother stares down at the table.

"Might as well let him move all my stuff. It'll be such a hassle for the two of us."

"What about paying for your books and supplies? And your meal card? Did you tell him you still need money for all that too, or did he forget already?"

"I'll take care of it," Sarah says in a raised voice.

Her mother gets up from the table. She puts the salad dressing in the refrigerator, then slams the door closed. Sarah starts loading the dishwasher.

"Nothing's going to change, Sarah Marie."

"What?" Sarah turns around, crunching her eyebrows.

"Just because he feels like being a father all of a sudden doesn't mean anything's going to change for good. You can't depend on him."

Sarah continues to rinse the dishes. She stacks them on the counter. They make loud clanking noises, but she doesn't care. She should've just told her father it was OK. After all, it is what *she* wants to do. Why should she have to bother asking her mom?

"Is he bringing the girlfriend?"

"I don't know if anyone's coming with us," Sarah snaps, even though she does.

"It's a real shame. All that man does is disappoint you time and again. Probably spending all kinds of money on someone half his age along with her kids."

"You don't know that anymore than I do." Sarah takes the dirty frying pan off the stove and scrubs it.

"Sarah Marie, if your father really wanted anything to do with you, he'd do more than these once or twice a year stunts. You need to get on with your life."

Sarah's so mad she can't even look at her mom. As if her dad were an old boyfriend she should have gotten over by now. She knows there's no way her mother can understand.

"You can't make people over," she says. "You're always trying to change people or hoping they'll change, but you can't change anyone."

Sarah shuts off the faucet and quickly dries her hands. Then she yanks the garbage bag from the can and slams it on the floor. She ties the ends together real tight and scowls at her mom: "You don't know what's in his heart anymore than I do." She storms out the door to the garbage cans, dragging the big black bag behind her.

Our parents' divorce can easily cause us all kinds of guilt feelings. Maybe you blame yourself somewhat for it, thinking you could have done something to prevent it. Or perhaps you feel you're being disloyal to the parent you're living with because you want a relationship with the parent who moved out, especially if your residential parent is having a tough time of it. Having younger siblings can increase guilt feelings as well, putting you in the difficult position of deciding how much of your own life should be sacrificed in order to care for them. How can we know when our guilt is justified and when it isn't?

Let's look at some definitions. When you think of situations causing guilt, what do you think of? Cheating on an exam? Lying about something important? Taking advantage of someone? All these instances warrant "justified guilt." Our moral sensor is working correctly, and our guilt feelings are based on reality. We are correct in assessing that we—or someone else—has done something wrong.

However, our moral sensor can overreact and cause us to feel unwarranted or false guilt, where our sense of right and wrong becomes very confused. This guilt often fuels unrealistic expectations of ourselves and persuades us to relate to others in unhealthy ways. It is ultimately self-destructive, because it encourages us to feel responsible for situations that are not our responsibility or are out of our control. This false guilt is what we'll explore in this chapter: the guilt we feel when we haven't done anything wrong.

In labeling her desire to have her father take her to college as "selfish," Sarah was feeling false guilt. She had every right to give priority to her wishes over those of her mother. Yet, Sarah felt as if she was doing something wrong. She assumed responsibility for her mother feeling "left out," even though they had already discussed her coming to visit during Parents' Weekend.

If you're trying to determine what type of guilt your parents' divorce may be causing you, try this exercise.

1. **Fill out the sentences that apply:**
   1. "The divorce is all my fault because _____."
   2. "I did a bad thing by _____."
   3. "If only I had _____, then the divorce probably wouldn't have happened."
2. **Journal your "uncensored" thoughts and feelings, expressing how these sentences relate to your parents or your family situation.**
3. **Now, look objectively at what you've written. Imagine someone else telling you these very thoughts and feelings. Would you conclude that this person is having unrealistic expectations of him/herself and therefore feeling false guilt? Explain.**
4. **Does your journal entry contain feelings of being "no good" or "defenseless"? If so, highlight these sentences with a marker. How much of your journal entry is composed of highlighted sentences? (These sentences indicate shame.)**

It's easy to confuse guilt with shame.

Guilt is about what we do to cause an offense, shame is what we feel when we more or less *are* the offense. Shame makes us feel as if we're no good, unworthy, or unable to do anything right. It may also make us feel defenseless.[3]

The false guilt associated with my parents' divorce haunted me well into my thirties. Most of the time, however, I didn't even recognize my feelings as guilt because I was so caught up in denial, fighting the fact that the divorce meant one big loss for my entire family. For a long time, it was easier for me to feel false guilt than to confront this loss, because the guilt let me feel that I was in control and able to change things when I really couldn't.

- Reconsider the situation prompting your feelings of false guilt and self-blame. What is it that you're assuming responsibility for?
- Does that responsibility really belong to someone else? If so, whom?
- In what ways might this person be choosing not to be responsible?
- What choices is he or she making instead?
- Reconsider this same situation. What makes it unrealistic to think you can control it?
- Since your parents' divorce, do you find yourself taking on too much responsibility at home as well as in your personal life? If so, in what specific way(s) has your life changed?

I fed myself repeated "if only" thoughts regarding my mother which nurtured my false guilt. When I was a preteen, I told myself things like, "I shouldn't be fighting with my brother so much, it's holding Mom back, and prevents her from doing what she wants to do because I'm being bad." I failed to see that my mother was responsible for improving her life. Moreover, I focused on her loss so much that I gave myself the impossible task of trying to make up for it through my achievements.

- Journal your "if only" thoughts or feelings regarding your parents' divorce without censoring them.

---

[3] See Chapter Two, "Shame," for further exploration.

- What is the goal of your "if only" thoughts?
- Is this really a goal that you can obtain, or are you only setting yourself up for repeated failures?

"If only" thoughts lead us down a path of self-deception. They never lead to real satisfaction or peace but keep us stuck in the same unfulfilled place. Like the person who centers his or her life on always having the best clothes or the best sports car, being the most popular or the best athlete, living life according to "if only" thoughts only leads to unhappiness because we never can obtain "enough."

Living my life according to "if only" thoughts instead of working through my false guilt created even bigger problems for me. I began to live inside my mother's skin and not my own. Sometimes, I didn't even know what my own viewpoints were and what I really wanted out of life because I was so entrenched in her skin.

- Is your way of handling your guilt feelings working? Or has it snowballed into bigger problems? If so, describe your dilemma(s).
- What losses has your parents' divorce brought to your life?
- Are you choosing to feel guilt and self-blame instead of facing and accepting these losses?

With my mother, I was caught in the dilemma of not knowing where to draw the line, i.e., what I "owed" her and what I "owed" myself. I wanted to live in a way that was right and loving for both of us, but I had great difficulty reaching that balance. I found myself often acting in one of two extremes: either disregarding my feelings and needs and doing only what my mother wanted, or reacting out of anger and refusing to acknowledge or consider her opinions at all.

Sarah has this same difficulty. At first, she considers only what her mother wants and takes responsibility for her mother feeling left out, even though she's attending Parents' Weekend. Only after Sarah gets angry does she consider her own wishes in the matter.

- Do you ever find yourself reacting in extremes with either or both of your parents, either doing all they want you to do or doing the exact opposite, just to rid you of false guilt?
- How could you have approached it in a way that was more considerate of everyone's wishes?

- Have you moved out of your parent's house or to a different state, thinking this would rid your false guilt? What happened? Did it rid you of your false guilt?

Neither doing only what my mother wanted nor completely disregarding her desires was the solution to my false guilt. Neither response ever felt right, because it remained a "reactionary" response. What worked for me was being straightforward about my desires and needs while stating them without resentment or anger. Oftentimes, my mother readily accepted my side, even wholeheartedly supported it. If she persisted in disagreement, then my task was to empathize and acknowledge her feelings. Sometimes, I had to come right out and ask my mother why it was so important to her for me to do this or that. These questions helped me better understand her, and they helped her compromise at times as well.

- What could you do (and not do) to relate and communicate better with your parents?

Now, let's look back at your first journal entry in this chapter and reconsider it in light of everything we have just explored.

1. **What corrections do I need to make in my way of thinking?**
2. **What incorrect assumptions and conclusions am I making?**
3. **What truths and convictions do I need to hold on to instead?**
4. **Are there thoughts and feelings that cause me to take on too much responsibility and feel false guilt?**
5. **Are there facts or truths I need to realize about this situation?**

If you're having trouble completing the last two questions, perhaps my answers to them might help you get started.

4. "How can I think about moving away and leaving Mom after all she's done for me? It just doesn't feel right. I feel like Dad, abandoning her all over again. It hurts me to know that she is alone. And, if I

move away, she'll be even more alone: no one there to protect her at night and watch over her if she gets sick. I should be the one there to do that. After all, she's done it for me my whole life. I feel so selfish, like I'm doing something really wrong. Mom will feel sadder and lonelier, and it'll be all my fault. Mom has sacrificed so much for me and now I have something she doesn't and likely never will. How am I supposed to enjoy my new married life plus move out of state, knowing I can't give Mom back all that she gave me?"

5. "Only Mom and/or Dad can take responsibility for the choices they made and are making now. Their lives are in their hands, not mine. I cannot live their lives for them, nor can I rescue them and give them back what they lost either. I am not abandoning my mom by moving away. I will be seeing her on holidays and just to visit. And she'll be visiting me too. She will not be completely alone if I leave. She has all her friends and the rest of the family.

"I'm doing nothing wrong by moving away. Quite the contrary. By getting married and moving out of state, I'm becoming the person God wants me to be and fulfilling God's plan. God is the ultimate master of my life. God wishes me to be at peace, free from the emotional burdens of sin, not in codependent relationships with my parents.

"Mom is responsible for claiming her own life and making it a happy one, just like I am responsible for making my life happy. I cannot live Mom's life for her, nor can I be responsible for her choices and happiness.

"My obligation is to try to be the best daughter I can, but I don't owe Mom my life in return for all the sacrifices she's made for me. Motherhood is a gift from God. My life is a gift from God. It is to God that I owe my life."

Are you facing a big decision in your life? Maybe you're considering going away to college, or taking a job, or pursuing graduate school in a state far from home. You know these are good opportunities for you, but you may feel that all-consuming feeling of unresolved, false guilt that says you're being selfish by leaving home. Perhaps you feel pressured to follow the career your mother and/or father want for you, since you want to give them the happiness they've missed out on in marriage. Maybe you're even considering marrying someone or entering religious life just for this reason.

Feelings of false guilt may become especially intense when we're faced with a decision that's good for us, but one that isn't what our parent(s) wants for us. Choosing to do what's best for our parents at the expense of doing what's right and best for ourselves ultimately puts us in the position of "parenting our parents." That is a very unhealthy position, and it will only encourage unhealthy relationships with them.

- How is your false guilt preventing you from making the decisions about your future that are best for you?
- Is false guilt causing you to take too much responsibility for your relationships with your parents?
- Consider the short- and long-term decisions that are causing your false guilt:
  a. What decisions cause you false guilt?
  b. What competing choices do you face?
  c. What do you want to do?
  d. What does God want you to do?

In the midst of false guilt, you may not give much thought to what God wants you to do. Leaving little room for God in my life allowed false guilt, as well as unawareness of God's plan for me, to linger way too long. When faced with the decision of getting married and moving out of state, my false guilt became so invasive that I needed to draw on a strength outside of and far greater than myself. I turned to God for guidance. Through prayer, I gradually found reassurance, leading me to the right course of action as well as freedom from feelings of guilt.

This struggle served as an important "wake-up call." I was reminded of how much I needed God's help in order to let go of being consumed by the guilt that kept me locked in a relationship for which I took responsibility that wasn't mine. At the same time, unrealistic expectations of myself kept me from seeing that God has a special purpose for all of us which, for me at this time, meant choosing life and love and freedom. This guilt did not begin to lessen until I sensed who God was calling me to be. Only then did my direction in life become apparent. I had to accept and trust that God truly loved me before I found the strength to follow this path and let go of unhealthy ways of relating.

I knew deep down that my decision to get married was right and willed by God because it was a call to love—to love my spouse and myself, which in turn would allow me to love others much more fully. Following this call required me to find the courage to take a risk and make changes, both in how I related to my mother and in lifestyle. However, it was a step that God was nudging me to take because it was a step toward growth and growing up, one in which I said "yes" to life and "moving on."

- Do you believe that God wants to help you overcome your guilt feelings?
- Are guilt feelings and their subtle "persuasions" keeping you from growing as a person?

As I wrestled with my false guilt, I began to see it as a struggle between good and evil. This outlook helped me to control it better and to stay committed to the "right path." I had never given much thought to being in the "grip of evil" before, but it is the best explanation I can give for the suffocating confusion that tormented me. My thinking prevented me from realizing and fulfilling God's plan for me in that it led me to believe I was responsible for other people's choices and happiness. My good intentions would prey upon my sympathy and compassion for my mother. My only defense against being devoured by this was through God's help.

- Consider again the decisions that cause you false guilt. What unhealthy thoughts and decisions might you be led to?
- How else might you be tempted?
- Are your friends a positive or negative influence on your feelings of false guilt?
- Do what they say, or the examples they set with their parents, make you feel too responsible (or not responsible enough) with your parents?
- Despite possible good intentions, what do your parents say or do that encourages your false guilt?

God wants us to discover the divine will and plan for our lives because that is what is best for us and ultimately brings us true peace and joy. We cannot reap these benefits if we're so guilt-ridden that we surrender to others the choices we need to make for ourselves.

CHAPTER FOUR

Grief

I roll to the opposite side of my bed. The front of my nightshirt is soaking wet. I grab it and fan away some of the perspiration that's poured out of me because of eating all those cookies.

I can't keep doing this. I sit up slowly. My stomach is one huge bulge. I probably gained five pounds.

I don't want to admit it, but I'm still not over Eric. This is going to be harder than I thought, the hardest thing I've ever had to do. I never believed he'd break up with me. Why do the men in my life always end up leaving me?

I look over at the picture of Jesus hanging above the stereo, a picture Mom put up one day without asking me. It's a "regular" picture of him, just sitting there with a beard and hair down to his shoulders, like one you'd see in a yearbook. I wish he went to my high school, or that he was a guidance counselor or someone I could interview for the school paper. I'd ask him all kinds of questions so I could understand why God let me care about Eric, only to take him away. I look at the picture and remember how Jesus was betrayed and crucified. I keep staring at the picture, thinking about the suffering Jesus underwent. And how he accepted it.

Images of the way Eric had his arms around Julie and how they were laughing flash my mind. Tears fill my eyes. Maybe he'll change his mind, realize he's made a mistake. Three months probably isn't long enough.

Tears begin to fall. "Help me God," I whisper, believing that if I stare long and hard enough at Jesus, God will somehow reach through him, and help me. I cry harder, shut my eyes tight. I feel like someone is sticking a knife right through me and sucking out my insides.

I repeatedly avoided grieving the losses associated with my parents' divorce for one obvious reason: my parents were still alive, so there still was the chance for our relationships to be renewed and made strong somehow. Therein lies the unique challenge to our grieving experience as children of divorce: clarifying our loss.

> Our grief is often delayed, if not "frozen," because our losses are rarely clear-cut. They are characterized, instead, by the absence of finality.

While our parents experience a finality to their lives together when they divorce, we don't. Our parents still remain our parents, and our need for loving relationships with them remains.

When my parents separated, I was very confused about the nature of the losses in my life. I had many questions about the changes: When and how often would I be seeing my dad? Was he ever going to move back? If not, and I moved to where he was, would it enable us to have a closer relationship? Added to this were concerns about other possible changes: Would we have to move to a smaller house? If so, would I be going to a new school and have to make all new friends? Did this mean I would have to choose a college that was closer to home? Nothing seemed certain anymore.

- Consider all the changes in your life that have resulted from your parents' divorce.
- Write them down in a left column in your notebook.
- Place a check mark to the left of the ones that have been most problematic for you.
- In a right column, note the losses, if any, that have resulted from those changes. (Include losses that directly involve your parents [e.g., not having as much time to talk with your mother because of her new boyfriend] as well as those that don't [e.g., not spending as much time with your friends because you have to work more hours].)

- Let us look at the losses in the right-hand column more closely. Differentiate between them:
  a. Are there losses I can improve in some way?
  b. What can I do to improve them?
  c. Are there losses I cannot do anything about and simply have to grieve?
- Are any of your losses unmanageable or paralyzing because you are unwilling to do what's required to try and improve them?

This exercise will make you more aware of the losses you may need to recognize and accept as "final," even though they may involve a family member who's still alive. The more we can grieve these losses, the further along we will move toward healing.

My most difficult losses concerned my father. They were losses that caused me great confusion and therefore difficulty in grieving. I sometimes found myself on a roller coaster ride where I'd have high hopes only to have them squashed. My dad would visit or I'd visit him, and I'd be so excited about spending time with him, only to realize how far he had moved on in his life without me. It shouldn't have shocked me, but it did because I hadn't moved on. I reacted, not by grieving these realities, but by becoming even more preoccupied with him. Although thousands of miles apart, my father continued to have a major influence on my actions and how I thought of myself, and I was always aware of his presence in my life.

- Have you ever felt "frozen in time" as a result of your parents' divorce?
- How has your preoccupation with someone or something you've lost, as a result of your parents' divorce, kept you stuck?
- In what areas of your life have you had difficulty moving on?
- In what ways are your mom and dad in and out of your life?

So what is grief anyway? It is defined as "deep and poignant distress caused by or as if by bereavement," according to the tenth edition of *Merriam Webster's Collegiate Dictionary.* Perhaps you've heard

of the five emotional stages of grief that persons go through following a serious loss. According to Dr. Elizabeth Kübler-Ross, they are:
denial (and isolation), anger, bargaining, depression, and acceptance.
This research may be useful as a general guide in understanding grief.
It lets us know these reactions are "normal" and part of the healing
process. Like me, however, you might find that you do not move
through the stages in exact order. You may experience them more as
fluid phases that surface and repeat themselves.

> We all grieve in different ways and move through grief at dif-
> ferent rates.

One of the most important rules of thumb is to avoid putting
yourself on a timetable for resolving your grief. Avoid comparing
yourself to others in this regard as well. We all wrestle with different
circumstances that may either help us or work against us in the grieving process.

It's also essential to distinguish our wishes from our hopes, as
wishes prevent us from grieving what we need to grieve. While there
was nothing wrong with my desire that my dad and I would be re-
united someday, I failed to consider the facts surrounding this desire,
namely, that he wasn't looking for any job opportunities in my home-
town, nor did he express any interest in doing so. Instead, he was
getting more and more settled in his new locale. To hold on to this
desire, therefore, meant holding on to a "wish," not a "hope."

> A wish is just a desire, whereas a hope has some basis in real-
> ity to it. Hope contains some truth toward which we can ob-
> jectively aim our faith.

We can carry this pattern of "wish making" into our dating relationships. In the vignette, for example, it's unlikely that, after three
months, Eric will change his mind about the breakup. In addition,
his having a new girlfriend whom he seems to be happy with makes
this even more unlikely. To think that he'll suddenly decide he's made
a mistake about the breakup is to hold on to a wish, not a hope.

- What wishes are you holding on to?
- What makes them unrealistic?

Oftentimes, our attitudes about sadness or sorrow prevent us from grieving. I have met many boys and young men of divorce who resist crying or feeling sad, especially in front of their male friends. Perhaps you've kept your feelings of grief deep down inside, too, because admitting them to others causes you too much embarrassment or makes you feel "weak." While it's not always easy to give in to our vulnerability, we must let ourselves feel the sadness somewhere if we want to move through it and heal.

- What is your attitude about crying and feeling sad about your parents' divorce?
- Does your "family background" encourage you to grieve or not?
- With whom do you feel safe enough to express your sorrow?
- What other outlets do (could) you have for your grief (e.g., keeping a journal, support groups, prayer, etc.)?
- Are you trying to shortchange your grief in seemingly healthy or normal ways (e.g., overachieving in school or sports)?
- Have you been channeling your grief in unhealthy ways (e.g., excessive use of alcohol, other drugs, food, sex) instead of confronting it head-on?
- Are there any relationships or activities that you cling to because not doing so would bring you face-to-face with your grief?

Overeating, the escape mentioned in the vignette, does not minimize grief or make it go away. Not only that, it leads to another problem, weight gain, that only adds disappointment to an already disappointing situation. We cannot avoid or cut short grief. Attempting to do so only means the grief will haunt us in other, likely worse, ways.

> We all need to find an outside source of strength, not escape, to help us move through grief.

For some, it may be talking with a trusted friend or counselor. For others, it might be joining a support group or nurturing a relationship with God.

- Who and/or what can you repeatedly turn to in your moments of sadness?
- Who and/or what have been the most helpful outlets to you?

Prayer has been essential to my healing, whether in the form of formal prayers, the rosary, or sitting alone in church and listening. Such moments of reflecting on God's presence in solitude are when the Holy Spirit has often spoken to me, either leading me to an insight or giving me that extra grace needed to carry my sadness. When grief has prevented me from sleeping at night, I have gone to my desk, where I keep a picture of the Sacred Heart of Jesus. Sometimes I've talked to him as if he were a real person sitting there. At other times, I have simply looked into the eyes of Jesus to get a sense of how much he loves me. I have always found my burdens lifted because I knew Jesus was right there, knowing my feelings and struggles. Bringing him into my hurts has never failed to lift them. It doesn't make my problems disappear, but it has always given me the strength to carry them.[4]

As children of divorce, we are likely to be cheated out of our grieving. Some persons may be oblivious to or refuse to acknowledge our grief, including our parents, especially since divorce is so prevalent. Nor do we have wakes, funerals, or acknowledged periods of mourning, like those losing loved ones to death. Moreover, we may feel pressured to "get over it," so we don't burden our friends with our sorrow or with our problems in the dating arena.

- Do you share your grief with Jesus? If so, what difference has it made in your life? If not, what holds you back from doing so?
- What influences cheat you out of your grief? Consider world tragedies that you might give more importance to, as well as the responses family and friends give to your grief.

We need to respect and honor our need to grieve and move at our own speed no matter what influences may be working against us. We

---

[4] In Chapter 11, "Surrendering to God," I explore the importance of a life of prayer more fully.

owe it to ourselves, especially if we want to make good decisions that are free of unresolved grief. Even though the circumstances surrounding your parents' divorce may not be as bad as someone else's, or even if someone close to you has lost a parent through death or is suffering with a serious illness or physical disability, you still need to own and acknowledge your own grief.

While tending to our grief, it is also important to take our minds off it at times and appreciate the blessings we do have right here and now. It's easy to forget or ignore other gifts in our life when weighed down by sorrow, but we need to recognize what is good to make room for even more good.

- What gifts are you thankful for?
- How might God's light be trying to penetrate your life as a result of your parents' divorce?
- What opportunities for greater understanding have your parents' divorce presented you with?
- How have your values changed or been strengthened?

Gaining a positive attitude can only come from staying focused on the growth opportunities that grief provides us. Jesus rose to new life only after accepting suffering and death on the cross. In a similar way, we gain strength and peace far greater than ever imagined if we can rise to the challenge of accepting and working through our grief in positive ways. If we run from this challenge and trick ourselves into thinking we can escape our grief, we will pay dearly. There's a price either way; I hope you choose the one that will truly benefit you in the end. Embrace your grief, and God will work wonders in your life.

Notes

CHAPTER FIVE

Anger

Nick checks his watch again. He tells himself not to take his mother's lateness as an insult. He must act nonchalantly; it's the only way to win this game. He brings his hand up to his face and breathes into it. His breath still smells like *Jack Daniels™*. He takes a couple more mints and pops them in his mouth.

Fifteen minutes pass. He hears the voice of her new boyfriend, Richard, followed by his mom's laughter as they step into the kitchen. Nick quickly raises the volume of the TV with the remote control. His mom and Richard talk with Nick's sister, Julie. Nick continues facing the TV. He hears his mom excuse herself to go to the bathroom.

"You must be Nick." Richard steps into the family room.

"Yes, I'm Nick." He lowers the volume with the remote. He doesn't want his mother to make a scene over it.

"Pleased to meet you." Richard extends his hand. Nick shakes it. The salesman type, he thinks. At least he'll be easy to snow. They start talking about cars and Nick's major at college. After a few minutes, Nick's mom steps into the room. She's dressed completely in white. White sweater and pants, even white stockings. Nick laughs to himself, thinking of his mom as the Virgin Mary.

"Hello, Nick," she says, heading to the bar. She fixes herself a vodka and tonic, then sits down next to Richard.

"Oh, I wonder how my stocks did today." She picks up the folded newspaper next to Nick's books. "I didn't even get a chance to read the paper yet." Nick looks back at the TV.

"So, you're taking statistics?" Richard nods at the books. "That was one of my favorite classes."

Nick answers him, pretending to be polite. His thoughts drift to Jennifer. He remembers the way she always smiles whenever he enters a room and the stacks of romantic cards she's given him. He doesn't feel guilty about not feeling the same way. After all, it's about time someone appreciates him.

"So, no date tonight?" His mom puts down the newspaper.

"No. I have a girlfriend, but I don't talk to her every night. It's not that serious."

"Well, you never know," his mom says. "These things need to stand the test of time. Just remember, no one out there's going to be perfect."

Richard makes his way to the bar, pours himself a drink, then leaves the room. Nick's mom stops talking and so does Nick. He's not about to play into her game. He knows she uses his girlfriends as topics for her own advantage. She shifts back and forth in her seat. Nick hopes he's making her nervous.

"No one out there's going to be able to fulfill all your needs," she adds.

He nods, then looks away, keeping his face expressionless. He can't pretend he's that naive. This isn't about what she expects anymore.

"But if you can get about ninety percent of your needs fulfilled, then you might have something."

"And what in the world didn't Dad do for you?" Nick feels like saying. He gets up from the chair and stands against the bar. He's heard about all the advice he can bear. His time is too valuable. He plants his hands on the counter, grips the edge tight. "So, what made you divorce Dad, anyway?"

She sips her drink. "Oh, that's a long story."

"I have time."

She looks down at her glass.

"He asked you to go to counseling. Why didn't you? Why didn't you do anything to try and make things work? That's pretty lame, you know." Tears start filling his eyes, but he doesn't stop them.

She spins her glass.

Nick starts to feel bad for how uncomfortable he's making her, but then he catches himself. The silence is probably just her way of manipulating him.

She looks at him. "I did the best I could."

"I don't believe that."

"Maybe I shouldn't even visit like this. Maybe it's best for you and your sister if I just stay away for good."

She wants him to cross that line so much it's pitiful. "And what kind of a mother are you? All you care about is your new boyfriend."

"There's always the future," she says in a calm, matter-of-fact voice. She looks out the window.

And how he wants to believe that. He curls his fingers into fists. "Well, if you keep acting the way you've been acting, neither Julie nor I are going to want to have anything to do with you."

"I've been having some problems of my own."

"That's a copout."

Richard returns. "How are we all doing in here?"

"Are you ready?" Nick's mom gets up and steps toward him.

"It's your soul, Mom."

Richard takes her coat from the kitchen chair and helps her put it on. Then he flashes Julie the palm of his hand. They head toward the back door without looking at Nick.

"You're not going to ruin my life," Nick yells. He picks up her empty glass and throws it at her feet. Glass shatters on the floor behind her. "You go to the people who use you and push away the people who love you."

They slam the door behind them. This time, Nick fights his tears.

What about anger? Are you upset with your parents because their divorce has brought all kinds of problems into your life that you're in no way responsible for? Do you blame them for your inability to achieve as before or for your failed dating relationships? Does anger, at times, make you want to have nothing to do with either one of them ever again?

Anger is a normal and healthy reaction to our parents' divorce. It protects us and lets us know when we've been hurt, betrayed, or wronged. On the shadow side, anger prevents healing, clouds perspectives, and controls us. When not channeled properly, it becomes life-taking, not life-giving.

Nick's anger convinced him of the worst about his mother. It prevented him from looking deeper to better understand other, and perhaps more correct, explanations for her behavior. He was caught in distrust, and therefore unable to salvage any relationship with her.

- When has your anger caused you to make incorrect assumptions about someone?
- When faced with a distressing situation you can't control, how often do you respond with anger?
- Has your anger over your parents' divorce ever taken hold of your life?
- Has it caused you to say or do things you later regretted?

It's easy to give ourselves over to anger when experiencing the hurts of our parents' divorce. After all, we're often the "forgotten victims" in the mix. Anger is also the one emotion that can seduce us into a sense of feeling in control.

> Anger gives us that temporary "high," a short-lived burst of energy, making us feel powerful and strong. In reality, this conclusion couldn't be further from the truth.

I carried anger inside me for a long time. I didn't want to do anything at home or at school that would cause my mother to be more upset or stressed. I covered up my feelings and tried to be the "perfect daughter" with my father also. I knew he was struggling to get his own life back together after he left home, and I wasn't about to add to his disappointment. I was afraid that expressing my hurt and anger toward him might cause him to push me out of his life permanently. I wasn't about to risk that.

Then, in my early twenties, when a serious relationship I was in started to fail, my anger came gushing out like a faucet. I took all my anger out on my boyfriend (whom I'll refer to as "Eric"). I was angry with him both for failing to be the boyfriend I needed him to be and for not "filling the void" created by my parents' divorce. Deep down, I expected him to replace my father and, in so doing, take away the emptiness.

- Are you more quick to express or repress your anger?
- If the latter, what do you fear might happen if you express your anger?

- What else influences you to repress your anger?
- Are you involved in a relationship in which you're expecting the other person to "right the wrongs" caused by your parents' divorce?
- Is there a part of you that hopes this person will take your father's or mother's place, giving you back what was lost?
- Have you ever found yourself overreacting in anger at your boy/girlfriend or another close friend when he or she has failed to meet your expectations?
- Did you later realize that the "punishment didn't fit the crime"? What happened?
- Looking back on these situations, might you have been releasing pent up anger at your parent(s)?

It was impossible, of course, for Eric to "right the wrongs" of my past. However, instead of accepting that reality and feeling its pain, I lashed out at him because that was far easier than feeling what I most needed to feel: grief. Anger became my escape. It gave me a false sense of being "in control." It was false in that I was not operating from a sense of who I was and what I wanted and believed in. I was merely responding with the same anger I saw when my parents fought. I also feared becoming victimized, as I felt both my mother and I had been when my dad left. In her book, *The Courage to Change: Empowering Your Life from the Inside Out*, Marilyn Gustin describes this experience of being victimized:

> Victimizing events usually leave us feeling helpless. We feel that we have, after all, nothing to say about what happens to us. We may feel trapped. We may feel betrayed or abandoned…or we may experience a kind of despair and give ourselves over to helplessness.[5]

As my relationship with Eric deteriorated, I got so caught up in my unresolved, residual anger that I could see little else. I ended up giving him ultimatums, pushing him away before he had the chance to leave me. I was not about to be rejected by Eric like I had seen my

---

[5] Marilyn Gustin, *The Courage to Change: Empowering Your Life from the Inside Out*, Liguori, MO: Liguori Publications, 1996, p. 10.

mother rejected, like I felt my own father had rejected me. Not only did I need to take responsibility for my feelings, I also needed to focus on what I could control, both with Eric and my father. It was the only way to disown my victimhood. With Eric, I could control whether or not I dated him. I could also date other guys with whom I might have a more satisfying relationship. With my dad, I could try to get to know him better, more fully understand his limitations, and therefore not take them as a personal rejection. I could also respond with forgiveness.

Nick had the same challenge with his mother, but he wasn't even open to hearing what she had to say about her problems. It was precisely this information that may have set his anger free. His anger, and refusal to give his mother the benefit of the doubt, kept him stuck in misery.

- Do you feel victimized in your relationships with either of your parents?
- If so, what do they do (or not do) that makes you feel this way?
- What has been your response to it?
- Consider what triggers your anger and feelings of being victimized, then respond to the following statements.
  a. Situations and actions/inactions that make me feel angry and victimized:
  b. I feel threatened (e.g., in my self-worth, for my safety, or survival):
  c. Decisions and actions I have control over in these situations:
  d. Understanding attitudes and insights that would minimize my bad feelings:
- What do you typically do when you're angry (e.g., yell and scream at a sibling, throw things, etc.)?
- Do you express your anger well, or do you respond in openly aggressive ways (i.e. getting in someone's face, crushing everyone in your path) or passive ways (i.e. staying quiet while thinking of ways to "get even")?
- We often lash out at persons we feel safe in confronting. Who usually are the scapegoats for your anger?
- Have you done hurtful things to yourself or others in attempts to get back at a parent who's hurt you (e.g., not

doing homework, using another as a scapegoat, etc.)? If so, what?

- Has this solved or aggravated your problem?
- Has your anger led to other (destructive as well as seemingly constructive) escapes in your life (e.g., drugs, alcohol, sex, as well as a preoccupation with achieving, sports, etc.)? If so, which ones?
- Instead of resorting to destructive outlets, what can you do to help yourself better control your angry feelings and prevent them from escalating (e.g., sports/exercise, writing in a journal, praying)?

Just like the tea kettle must release steam whenever it boils, we too need to get our anger out. But we have to do more than express it. We have to surrender to it and confront the hurt behind it, so much that it "breaks" us.

> We need to let ourselves cry and cry deeply. It is the only way to release the destructive energy of anger and get the disease out so that it stops suffocating and robbing us of our precious life.

Only then can we be led more deeply into ourselves, to acceptance of our woundedness. We need to own the woundedness behind our anger in order not to be controlled by it. At the same time, however, we also need to disown the anger and angry patterns of our parents. The following questions may help you to integrate the source of your anger into your life in a more positive, healthy way:

1. What are you most angry with your dad and/or mom about?
2. What mistake(s) has he or she made to cause you such anger?
3. How has this mistake wounded you?
4. How might God be using that mistake to help you grow?
5. What positive qualities could you allow the mistake to develop in you?
6. In what ways are you different from/similar to the parent who is causing you such anger?

- Have your parents given you a positive or negative example of how to handle anger? Explain.
- Do you view either of your parents as angry persons? weak persons?
- Do you think you might (subconsciously) copy or "act out" these characteristics in your relationships?
- Could you, instead, be trying to become the exact opposite of your parent(s) in this area?
- Might either of your parents be transferring anger at his or her "ex" onto you? If so, when have you noticed this happening?
- Have angry or aggressive outbursts been rewarded in your life?
- What friends and/or family members can challenge you to grow past your anger?

Accepting the loss of my father was the first step in resolving my anger. This included anger at myself, which was relentless and vicious. All I kept thinking was: "How could I have been so clueless to have believed for twelve years that Dad was going to come back and that my relationship with him would never change?"

I had to learn to befriend my woundedness, that part of myself that I hated and was so ashamed of, that rejected part of myself that would always be there.

> I had to discover the good aspects of my woundedness: the compassion it nurtured in me, an understanding of similar struggles in others, a ready identification with Jesus and his suffering on the cross.

In time, I grew to love this part of myself and see it as valuable.

- Has your parents' divorce caused you to feel angry at yourself?
- If so, what are you angry at yourself for?
- What positive qualities has your parents' divorce nurtured in you?
- What positive qualities could you allow it to nurture?

Facing this loss also allowed me to begin to know Jesus in a real way. I could no longer deny the Lord who was with me every day, no more than I could deny the weight of my hurt and anger. In those moments as I sat alone on the floor of my apartment, staring across the room at the wall, I saw the face of Jesus looking at me for the first time in a long time. And I heard a faint whisper, "Let me help you." During the days and weeks that followed, I learned to give Jesus that chance. I gradually turned my hurt and anger over to God, trusting and believing that I was loved by my divine father in heaven. My problem became one that Jesus shared with me and, together, we started a new journey. I no longer saw him as my adversary sitting far across the table from me. Instead, I met him as a friend who walked beside me, listening to me and helping me to let go, making room for God's Spirit to work.

Notes

CHAPTER SIX

Rejection

I don't know. I just don't understand Ellen," Katie's dad says. "Everything's been great between us these past few months, but now she tells me she's not sure if she'll ever get married again." He's been talking a long time. But not about Katie.

They've finished eating, and her father has already paid the bill. She hasn't seen him in over a month. It's the most he sees her now that he and her mother are divorced and he's moved into his own place.

"I don't know what she's worried about. It couldn't be money. She knows I make enough, even with all the alimony and child support your mother has gotten out of me. I could take better care of Ellen than that dud she was married to, that's for sure." He sips his coffee.

Katie remembers her birthday last month and how her dad didn't call or send her a card. He never forgot her birthday when her parents were married. She turns down the corners of her mouth, but a couple seconds later she notices him looking down at his coffee cup with a sad look all over his face. So she says, "You never know, she might change her mind. Maybe you just have to give her more time."

"Well, I'm not going to let any grass grow under my feet, that's for sure." He goes on to tell her about another woman, Sue, whom he might ask out. Katie glances around the restaurant, tries to make eye contact with the waitress.

"At least Sue doesn't have any kids," he says. "That's one thing

I'm not too crazy about with Ellen. If we'd ever get married, both her kids would have to live with us."

Katie stacks her silverware in the middle of her plate while he tells her about Ellen's divorce and all the problems she's having with her ex-husband. Katie feels like telling him she's not a marriage counselor, and that she could care less about this woman. But she figures it wouldn't make any difference.

Her Dad raises his hand to order another cup of coffee. "Want anything?" he asks her.

"No thanks," she says.

"I'll have another, please," he tells the waitress from across the room, pointing to his cup. She heads over to their table carrying a glass coffee pot, refills his cup then leaves. "Don't get me wrong," he continues, "in many ways, Ellen is very good for me."

Katie opens her Styrofoam™ container and takes another bite of her leftover cheesecake. Her dad hasn't just left her mom and moved out of the house. He's moved out of Katie's life too.

Have you felt rejected in any way since your parents' divorce? Maybe your father has remarried and is no longer giving you any money, instead, giving it to his new wife and her kids. You may even feel as though he doesn't consider you a part of his family anymore because he devotes almost all his time and attention to his "new family." Maybe he no longer does the "little things" he once did, like sending birthday cards, just as Katie experienced.

Your mother may be treating you differently as well. Perhaps she doesn't seem as interested in how you're doing in school or whom you're dating. Maybe she's not going to your basketball games or letting you bring a college friend home with you over spring break like you used to do because, she says, it's "too much" for her. Any of these actions can't help but cause one to feel rejected.

- What has your mom and/or dad done (or not done) since their divorce that makes you feel rejected and perhaps not loved anymore?
- How has your relationship with your parents changed since their divorce?

Letters were the primary way my father kept in touch with me after he left home. I was always thrilled to find a letter from him in the mailbox because it let me know he was still thinking about me. And the letters weren't just ordinary letters either, because he did share who he was, along with his guilt feelings and remorse in having left me. I felt fortunate to have a father who confided so much in me, and my compassion for him grew with each letter.

Yet, as the months and years passed, I felt more and more removed from his life. His letters became more focused on his world away from me. He always let me know I was welcome to visit him, but being over a thousand miles apart made our get-togethers infrequent. No matter how much we talked, it just wasn't the same as having him right there. I kept wanting and needing him to call me more often, see me more often, do the things that dads were *supposed* to do. That didn't happen, and I felt more and more rejected by him. As a result, I concluded that he didn't love me anymore and that maybe he never really did.

After the lunch with her father, Katie felt similarly rejected. Her father was so consumed with his dating problems that he never thought to ask Katie about what was going on in her life. He paid her so little attention during their time together that she couldn't help feeling as if he had divorced her along with her mom.

- What negative conclusions have you made about your parents because of the way they seem to be rejecting you?
- Putting these judgments aside, try to step into your parents' shoes. Think about their values, fears, shortcomings— the essence of who they are and aren't. Drawing on this information, write a description of each of them.
- What does your description show you about how well you know your parents?
- What important aspects of your parents do you still need to learn more about?

For many years I wrestled with the question, "Does Dad love me anymore?" I often felt that he did not, since that was the simplest way to explain my feelings of rejection, and one that encouraged me to hold on to them; however, during quiet moments when I was alone, I often heard a nudging voice deep inside telling me there was more to the picture. I didn't have enough facts about my dad, or at least not the right ones. So, whenever the holidays or summer vacation came around and I flew to visit him or he flew to visit me and my family, I tried as best I could to get to know him. That meant shelving what I needed and expected so I could discover who he really was instead. Not shelving these aspects of myself would have prevented me from seeing my father as a man with weaknesses and struggles, like us all. Because I was able to do this, my feelings of rejection lessened.

- How might your parents' limitations (as well as their attitudes, beliefs, and values) prevent them from loving you in the ways you need? Based on the following questions, jot down as many qualities as you can think of.
  a. What do I need Mom and/or Dad to be like?
  b. What *are* Mom and/or Dad really like?

> Realizing the true nature of our parents' love for us can be difficult because it involves realizing what they cannot do or provide for us.

This is often a scary and painful realization—one it's easy to ignore in order to put the responsibility for our happiness and well-being on them instead of on ourselves.

- Look back at your answer to the first question in this chapter. What can you do in these situations to try and get what you want (e.g., communicating your needs to your parents, reaching out in some way to them)?
- If not from your parents, where else can you get these needs met?

Taking charge of these situations at times requires us to let go of whatever we may feel "entitled" to receive from our parents. Thinking in terms of "entitlement" gets us nowhere, and only distracts us from pursuing the growth opportunities available to us.

When I took this step and did more on my own to get my needs met, I felt a sense of freedom like never before. I discovered who I really was and who I wanted to be. Gaining a sense of inner fulfillment and purpose, in turn, led to more growth. I stopped blaming my parents for not being "perfect" and accepted them as persons with limitations just like everyone else, including myself. I realized that if I wanted them to love and accept me for who I was, especially in the midst of my weaknesses and struggles, I needed to accept them in theirs as well.

- What weaknesses and struggles do you have that you hope others will accept with patience?
- What are your parents' weaknesses and struggles that you need to accept more readily?

Accepting my parents for who they are brought them closer to me. They began to reveal more of their real selves to me, along with their deeper feelings about the divorce. The more I could be with them in their pain, the more I allowed for a new and better relationship to grow between us. Instead of merely relating as parent and child, we grew in friendship. This gave me a deep sense of inner fulfillment and pride, because I had affected this change.

- Do any of your attitudes toward your parents show them that you don't want a relationship with them? If so, which ones?
- If not, what are you doing to meet your parents halfway (or more)?

Much of what I heard about the past, particularly from my dad, surprised me. He admitted to having financial problems after he left us. This kept him moving from state to state as he tried to establish a more stable career and financial position. He also expressed tremendous feelings of guilt. He knew he had been unfair to me, and that deep down he hurt a lot, feeling that he had failed me. While admitting he had made mistakes, he really didn't know what he could have done differently at the time. Once he expressed his feelings of sorrow and regret, I thought of how Jesus would respond if he were there listening. I knew Jesus would accept, have great compassion for him, and forgive him, and my heart was bursting to do the same. I was overwhelmed by the pain my father had been carrying with him for years, pain I had been totally unaware of.

> Hearing either parent's side doesn't make everything perfect;
> it furthers an understanding of the reasons behind his or her
> actions and inactions. It's the only way to discover the truth
> and "move on."

I came to understand that my father did love me, it just hadn't
shown itself where I had been looking. That didn't make his love any
less important or good, even though I had thought of it in that way.
I had focused on what he wasn't doing instead of what he was. Once
I realized this, I learned one of the most important and valuable lessons of my life: My dad wasn't there to meet every guy I dated, but he
was there to walk me down the aisle and pay for my wedding. He
gave of himself in the ways he felt were most important and in the
ways he could give best.

> People can only give their unique love, not our love nor any-
> one else's.

- Are you appreciative of the ways in which your parents
  might be trying, in their own way, to reach out and love
  you?

What happens if your parents aren't even trying to do a better
job? Are you supposed to excuse their shoddy behavior or justify their
mistakes? Certainly not. Nor should we honor dishonorable parents.
Rather, the challenge is first to see our parents for who they are (and
aren't) and not let our neediness or anger distort this reality. This
awareness won't make the hurt go away, but it should enable us to
take their "lack of parenting" less personally. We'll at least be in a
better position to see their behavior not as a reflection of their love
for us but, more accurately, as a reflection of who they are. The next
challenge is to find a positive way to incorporate this experience into
our own lives. Let it motivate you to reach out to your siblings or
other teens or young adults of divorce who are struggling. Allow it to
deepen your relationship with God. It may even inspire you to do
that much better of a job raising your own kids some day. The potential for good results is great.

Feeling rejected by our parents leaves us with two choices: We can either resent them for our feeling "cheated," or we can try to focus on the good that remains in our relationship. As in all other significant relationships, we'll need to find other ways to fulfill the needs that our parents can't or simply don't know how to meet.

I didn't want to live my whole life filled with such resentment and anger, nor did I want to carry these destructive attitudes into my relationships and let them rob the best of me. I wanted to grow and love myself and others better. The responsibility for this choice was mine and mine alone.

Only I was able to get past my feelings of rejection. So too with you. Do you care and value your life enough to rise to the challenge? If so, you will find that you will more likely grow more from that than from any other challenge in your life. My hope is that you give yourself that chance.

You owe it to yourself, and you owe it to your parents.

Notes

CHAPTER SEVEN

Rejection by God

I'm upstairs in my bedroom doing homework when I hear Mom and Dad yelling at one another downstairs in the dining room. I hear Dad raise his voice. I quickly close and lock my door. I walk to the window. Dishes clank. The dining room cabinet bangs shut. Mom and Dad start yelling again.

I look outside at our backyard, lit only by the lights above the garage. I wish I could climb out onto the ledge below my window, jump down to the ground, and run to the gazebo. But I know I can't without hurting myself. Besides, it's really cold outside and all my coats are downstairs. I look at my old wooden dollhouse, then King, our German shepherd, sitting in front of his doghouse, the flowerbed, our driveway, then over the hedges and into the neighbor's yard. Everything's still and dark. But I keep looking out the window anyway.

After ten minutes, the house gets quiet. They aren't yelling anymore. Where did they go? I walk back to the door, put my ear against it, and hear nothing. I want to open it, but I'm too afraid. I walk back to the window and look at the tall maple tree right in front of me, then higher at the dark night. "God," I whisper, "where are you?" I keep looking outside, but nothing changes.

More silence. I turn on my stereo and play my favorite song, *This I Promise You*. I try to listen to it, but I can't. Why isn't God doing something to help? I turn off the stereo. More silence. I change into my nightshirt and crawl into bed. I lie down and look out the window at the dark night, at the handful of stars scattered throughout it. How can God let them fight all the time like this? God knows how difficult it is to live with. I remember how I haven't spoken to Patty in a month. Is this God's way of punishing me for not forgiving her? Seems pretty harsh to me.

I pull the covers more tightly over my shoulders. I don't know what to think about God anymore. I thought he was supposed to love me.

Where is God in the midst of our pain? Why are the answers to our prayers sometimes delayed? Why do bad things happen to us, especially when we've done nothing wrong? How can a good, loving God allow for this?

Questions like these are likely the most difficult ones we'll ever ask in our faith journey. We long to have them answered, or at least to hear specific reasons for how God loves us yet allows us to experience tough problems resulting from our parents' divorce.

> If God doesn't give us adequate answers for understanding the mystery of our suffering, how are we supposed to respond to it in the context of faith?

For years, I made secret bargains with God. I wasn't about to let myself get hurt anymore, so before trusting God again, I wanted answers to why so many bad things were happening to me and my family. However, the more I struggled to figure out "why," the more confused I became.

What God was asking me to do was something radically different: to put on an attitude of faith, believing that God was working for my ultimate good even when it appeared that no one was listening. The first step was to let go of my need to have answers.

- What is happening in your family and/or personal life that makes you feel like God is rejecting or has deserted you?
- In what negative and/or positive ways has your struggle affected your faith in God?
- What questions and/or doubts do you have now that you didn't have before your parents' divorce?

- Based on your response to the preceding question, what does it reveal about your expectations of God?

What is especially pressing for us to understand in these situations is the connection between difficulties and God. I had always thought deep down that having God in my life and trying to live in a "right way" would spare me major difficulties and pain. As in the vignette, I kept searching for what I had done "wrong" when my parents separated and eventually got divorced. Such faulty reasoning presumes that God causes the difficulty, which is not the case. What God brings us is the ability to cling to God's very self which will strengthen us with the direction necessary to overcome our difficulties and hardships.

Drawing on our faith in God will help us overcome difficulties and make better choices, but it won't rid our lives of problems.

At times it may seem as though God is doing nothing to help us. I remember times when I've prayed, asking God for help in better handling a problem, only to find myself not led to any increased understanding or confidence. Can God still love us and seemingly delay answering our prayers?

As the girl depicted in the vignette, I didn't think so. I didn't understand how God could be helping me by seemingly doing nothing. Yet, even in those instances when my parents were fighting a lot and God wasn't "stepping in" to stop it, I was being helped. It just wasn't in the way I wanted and expected it.

God knows what is ultimately best for us, and is always working to move us toward a higher good. Oftentimes, our confusion and/or suffering is the very vehicle by which this is accomplished.

If God had answered my prayers as a young girl by making my parents tidy everything up instead of separating, I would not have grown in character in the way that I did; I would not have been drawn out of myself in the way that I eventually was; I would not have come to understand, to the extent that I do, the difficulties that are the rationale for this book; and I would not have experienced the calling to reach out and help you and thereby participate in a unique way in the body of Christ. No, God did not abandon me in my pain. When God seems to abandon us in our pain it is actually an invitation to draw us closer to Jesus.

- When has disappointment made possible new opportunities in your life?
- Consider failed dating relationships, not making a sports team, failing a class, not going to the prom with the guy/girl of your dreams. What windows opened in your life precisely because these doors were closed?
- How might your struggle with your parents' divorce be an invitation and a challenge to grow in character?
- What shortcomings in yourself can your suffering burn away?
- Has your struggle enabled you to understand, relate to, or empathize more fully with others? If so, explain.
- In what ways is your struggle challenging you to deepen your faith and trust in God? What do you think God is trying to say to you through it?
- Do you trust God more than your most trusted friend?
- Do you trust God more than yourself?
- If not, how might you begin to place more confidence in God (e.g., presenting your dilemma to a priest in confession or to God during prayer, reading books about faith, etc.)?
- What desires might God have for you in your struggle that differ from what you want?
- Instead of rejecting you, how might God be challenging you to embrace a better path for yourself?

I experienced a very difficult time in my early twenties when God challenged me to see a better path for myself. I was years into a dating relationship that wasn't working. My boyfriend and I were good friends but, as things got more serious, we began to fight about everything. Instead of seeing the red flags, I ignored them and made excuses for our problems because I feared losing him and being alone. Worse, I tried to change who I was in the process.

It was a vulnerable point in my life. I was unclear of my career goals, I wanted to live on my own but couldn't afford to, and I was not yet completely at peace with my parents. So I looked to my boyfriend to be the anchor in my life, even though he was not the right guy for me and I was not ready for a serious relationship. Still, I clung to the relationship, kidding myself into thinking I could fix it like a math problem.

God continued to tell me "no, no, no," but I ignored this inner voice because I feared going where it called me: to experience the grief of a breakup and to be "boyfriend-less"—a grief I sensed would unleash the unresolved grief I had with my father. At the time, I didn't understand why God was allowing yet one more area of my life to fall apart instead of giving me just this one "plank" to hold on to. I had touched despair, and knew I had to end the relationship.

When I finally mustered that courage, the pain was overwhelming. I spent evenings alone in my apartment just staring across the room, listening to music, unable to do much of anything else. I had never felt more alone, more scared, and more abandoned. Fortunately, this time I found enough strength to sit with the pain instead of running away from it.

> Accepting pain and trying to be patient with it is an invaluable lesson.

Sitting with the pain taught me the importance of being receptive to God's grace and direction. I learned that with God we are sometimes encouraged to "be" rather than "do." I did not have any particular peak experience of faith in those dark moments; it was more like God entering my life as a glimmer of soft light. As I opened my heart little by little each day, God gave me the strength and the will to move on, to find myself again, and gradually to make a better life for myself.

- Are you choosing to approach your struggle through the eyes of faith? If so, explain.
- If not, in what small way(s) might you begin to do so?

Had I not heard God's "no" in that relationship, I would not have discovered the far greater "yes" that followed. Not only did this "no" open a door through which I began to rely ever more on God as my anchor in life, it gave way to a "yes" that allowed me to find the inner strength needed to love myself. I came to see that even though I had to bear much pain in that relationship and its breakup, the experience was necessary in order for me to realize, finally, the extent of my weaknesses and my need to draw on a strength far greater than myself. Part of that learning involved sometimes relinquishing what I thought was best for myself. The "person" who did know me best and who had the perfect plan for me, instead, was God. In my stubbornness, fear, and reluctance to trust God, I got in the way of myself. I needed to learn to give my uncertainties and all I couldn't control over to God.[6]

- What uncertainties and fears do you need to hand over to God?
- What else are you trying to control that is better left in God's hands?

Another important point to realize about struggles is that not only are they essential to drawing us closer to God through Jesus, they also go hand in hand with God's gift of freedom to us. It is precisely because all of us have the ability to make bad choices that some of us suffer in the first place. In the vignette, my parents caused my distress by choosing to resolve their problems in a less than helpful way. They were making the bad choices, not God.

- Who are the ones responsible for making the choices that have led to your struggle?
- What bad choices have these persons made and/or are they making?
- What bad choices are you being encouraged to make as a result?
- In what specific ways do you need God to help you with this?
- Do you ask God to help you? If not, how might you start to do so?
- What are you clinging to in place of God's love (e.g., a

---

[6] In Chapter 11, I explore "Surrendering to God" more fully.

dating relationship, popularity, a job, sports, alcohol or drugs, sex, achievements)?
- In what way(s) may God be telling you "no"?
- Has God closed any "doors" in your life?
- In what ways might God be trying to redirect your energies?

The "no" of my failed dating relationship encouraged me to place my faith and trust in God. I needed to do this to open myself to grace and direction. I learned that God was not a coddling kind of God whose job it was to make me "feel good." Rather, I learned that God used my problem as a way to get my attention, to make me evaluate where my life was and wasn't going, and to let myself be led down the best path. God alone knew how to further my highest good. Time and again this required me to readily commit myself to what I discerned to be God's will. When I succeeded in doing so, my needs were met in ways I never imagined possible. God's protection was with me every step of the way, and I was never given more than I could handle.

- What (if anything) hinders you from being more open to God's grace and direction?
- How might God be trying to get your attention through your struggle?
- What is it that you need to reevaluate in your life?
- What might God be trying to get you to do differently?
- What can you do to open yourself more to God's will in your life (e.g., setting aside more time for prayer, attending Mass more often, reading the Bible or a spiritual book, joining a youth group, etc.)?
- What benefits might unfold in your life if you take this step?

In learning to accept our difficulties, we may also take great consolation in what Jesus showed us about suffering—the way we move to glory. Suffering taught him obedience to God, and completed his faith. So, too, can our hardships move us to a new, fuller life and increased strength of character.

Our walk in faith is a lifelong, uneven journey filled with valleys and peaks. At times, we may find ourselves sure of God's love for us while, at other times, we may question whether there's any goodness at all to be found. The essential outlook we need to have through it all is openness, especially in the midst of our difficulties.

> God works for good in our lives, but we have to be open to receive it.

Walking by faith will require us to take chances and go out of our comfort zones. It will not provide us with a security blanket behind which we can hide from the world and its troubles but will urge us to do something positive about our difficulties. Just as God didn't cause our parents' divorce, so he will never reject or abandon us in our pain. What God gives us is the greatest gift we could ever ask for: the presence of God's very self as we live with, move through, and grow from our difficulty. That, indeed, is what we need most. It will require us to place our very lives in God's hands. Once we do, we will find true healing and growth and a purpose in our pain.

CHAPTER EIGHT

Dating Relationships

I t's been fifteen minutes since we've left his firm's office party, and Eric still hasn't spoken to me. I know he's still miffed at how I got on his case last weekend for watching that baseball game on TV while we were eating dinner. It's been five months, I remind myself. He wouldn't break up with me now.

I hug my arms tight, look out the passenger window. He's never gotten this quiet with me before. Maybe this is going to be our last date. I try to relax, think of something else, but the silence won't let me. The music from the car stereo keeps pounding. It's as if it's trying to warn me that something bad is about to happen.

He takes the exit off the highway and turns left toward my house. I get a sinking feeling in my stomach. I force myself to breathe slowly. The clock on his dashboard says ten thirty. Why can't we just hang out at his apartment like we usually do? I tell myself this isn't really happening. He'll turn around pretty soon. Maybe he's just waiting for me to say something.

He goes up the driveway toward the back of my house. I shift back and forth in my seat. "Don't leave me like this," I say quietly to myself. My body starts to shake.

He turns his car around, faces it toward the back door, and stops. "Get a good sleep," he says, glancing at me, then back at the steering wheel.

"But it's only ten thirty. You never go to sleep before midnight."

"I told you I wanted to make it a short night," he says, still looking away from me. "I have to get a good night's sleep. I have a 7:00 a.m. golf match tomorrow with some clients."

Don't cling, I order myself. Don't beg. I unlatch my seat belt, then dig into my purse for my keys. I clench the cold metal pieces, let go of them, then dig for them again. He turns on the light above the front seat. "I'll talk to you later."

I can't believe he's doing this to me. I grab my keys, squeezing the metal points into my skin. I push until it hurts so bad I can't stand it, then I remove the keys from my purse. He turns off the light.

"Thanks again. I really enjoyed the party." I watch his turned face. He nods without looking at me. I slowly open the door. He adjusts the rearview mirror. I can't believe he's just taking off like this. How can he do this to me?

I put one foot on the pavement. He turns the headlights back on. I bite my top lip. More silence. I glance at the dark kitchen window, remember how Mom caved with Dad. I hear Dad's shouts, Mom's cries.

"I just don't know about this relationship anymore," I blurt out. He says nothing, continues to look away from me.

"I deserve to be treated better than this." I grab the inside door handle. "This just isn't working for me anymore." I swallow the gulp of air at the back of my throat.

"Look, it's late. I've got to get going," says the voice beside me. I hate the way he's blowing me off. He's so cool with how bad our relationship is, like it doesn't really matter at all to him. Maybe he really is thinking of breaking up. Maybe that'll be the next call I get from him, if he calls at all.

"I refuse to be treated this way. Maybe the other losers you dated put up with it, but I'm not going to." My voice is shaking. I force myself up from the seat, then grab the door with both hands. I can't believe I'm doing this. "This just isn't working for me anymore," I shout at him, then slam the door closed.

He takes off, peeling rubber, then speeds down the road. My body trembles as I stand there watching him leave. I look back at the dark kitchen window. I wish I hadn't said what I did, but at least this time I didn't lose.

✱

It wasn't until I got involved in my first serious dating relationship after college—twelve years after my dad left home—that the consequences of my denial of the problems from my parents' divorce reared their ugly head full force. I dated Eric not because we shared similar values and interests or complemented each other's personalities, but because he was like my parents in key ways. It was a relationship that enabled me to relive my problems with them. In particular, it gave me the opportunity to work through the loss of my father.

- Do you share values, interests, and life goals with your boy/girlfriend?
- Which don't you share? How important are the latter to you?
- Does your boy/girlfriend meet your most important needs? If not, which of your needs aren't being met? Is your boy/girlfriend capable of meeting them?
- Is he or she someone you can grow with? If so, in what ways?
- Are you with this person because s/he is "safe," i.e., someone you don't fear losing?

Most of the time, I was miserable with Eric, and we fought often. Still, something kept me in the relationship, thinking it was "right." The main reason it felt "right" or "comfortable," though, was because Eric enabled me to relive old patterns and ways of relating to my dad. I retraced the same emotional steps and made the same rationalizations and excuses. Instead of approaching my unhappiness as an opportunity to look deeper at who Eric was (and wasn't)—asking myself whether he would ever be able to meet my most important needs—I convinced myself that it was only a matter of time before he'd learn to love me in the ways I needed him to. This was an impossibility for Eric. He lacked the ability to do so.

I reacted to Eric in the same ways as I reacted to my father. I blamed "poor timing" for both of their inabilities to meet my needs. I told myself things like, "When Dad finds a job that's right for him, has fewer financial worries, and a girlfriend, then he'll be happier and take a greater interest in my life." With Eric, I told myself, "He just needs time. He'll learn how to love me better as time goes on."

As the years passed, my relationships with neither Eric nor my dad improved in the ways I had hoped; however, I still ignored their limitations because that would mean I would have to acknowledge that they couldn't meet my needs, and therefore I was "alone" in the world.

- Consider a situation when you were really disappointed about something your boy/girlfriend did or didn't do. How did you come to terms with it?
- Did you rationalize or make excuses for his/her behavior?
- Has it become a problem in your relationship?
- Does your boy/girlfriend have limitations that you don't want to admit? If so, what do you wish you could change about him/her the most?

> As difficult as it is, we need to step back and examine whether we're clinging to "wishes" or "hopes" in our dating relationships. We may want a relationship to work out so much that we hold on to wishes or false beliefs. A wish is only a desire, whereas a hope has some reality as to its fulfillment.

- What unfulfilled desires do you have in your dating relationship(s)?
- Are these desires wishes or hopes? Explain.
- Do you notice any patterns repeating in your life?
- Might you be transferring the unfulfilled wishes in your relationship with your parent(s) to your dating relationship(s)?

Sometimes my denial gave way to shame and self-reproach. Just as I had attributed my father's infrequent involvement in my life to my not having achieved enough, so I blamed myself for Eric's inability to meet my needs. "I shouldn't need so much attention," I'd tell myself. "Maybe if I wasn't so serious all the time, we'd get along better." Not only did I deny my needs, but I tried to change the very person I was. Eric, in essence, served as the magnifying glass that stood between my father and me, intensifying what was most difficult for me to accept about my dad and thereby bringing the pain of that relationship to the surface so I could work through it. I overreacted with Eric, at times resorting to ultimatums and threats to end the relationship, as shown in the vignette. The looming split with

Eric regurgitated a prior relationship. The looming split with Eric regurgitated the split with my father. I was restrained by fear that a past in which fighting and uncertainty led to my dad's painful leave might repeat itself. This caused me to leave Eric before he left me. It was my desperate attempt to "reverse" the outcome I had personally experienced with my dad and had also lived through with my mom.

In those moments, unresolved grief came back to haunt me. I felt like I was in a scary movie, only worse, because this was real. A foreboding feeling of doom consumed me, dark and heavy, and unlike any fear I'd ever had. Looking back, the only way I can describe it is that, in those moments, I was brought face-to-face with evil.

- Have you found yourself overreacting in anger or disappointment in your dating relationships? If so, journal these incidents.
- Try to look at these situations more objectively. Might they have scratched the surface of problems you have with your parents that you've been denying? If so, what are these problems?
- Do you relate to your boy/girlfriend in ways similar to your relating to your father or mother?
- Do you find yourself repeating similar patterns in both types of relationships (e.g., making excuses for them, attacking them verbally when you're angry)?
- Are your frustrations and disappointments the same in both?
- Journal your strongest feelings toward both men or women. Do you notice any important similarities?
- What is it that you lean on your boyfriend or girlfriend for?
- What can you do to meet these needs on your own?

I have met many young adults of divorce who have expressed similar fears as a result of their unresolved grief. They admit to fears of getting divorced themselves and even considerations of suicide when dating relationships have failed. One way in which some try to combat these fears is by choosing a boy/girlfriend who is "safe." This person is someone we don't fear losing, either because we're convinced he or she would never leave us or because it'd be "no big loss" if the person did leave. We can be controlled so much by unresolved grief that we resign ourselves to relationships that involve minimal emotional risk and hurt.

> Clinging to a dating relationship out of need rather than choice is a sign that you're looking for your boyfriend or girl-friend to give you what your parents did not give you.

While such relationships might last and even develop into stable marriages, how satisfying can they ultimately be? Equally important, can such a relationship really help us grow in the ways we need most?

Another problem that may surface in dating relationships and reveal unresolved problems with our parents is treating a boy/girl-friend as a "human rescue operation." In other words, we may feel a powerful urge to "save" the person we're dating. I was involved once in such a relationship. My boyfriend at the time (whom I'll call Steve) wasn't a "needy" person, nor was his life "a mess." However, when I met him, he had just lost his job. I took an interest in his job search and, as our relationship progressed, took it upon myself to call employers for him, bring him to networking functions, and rewrite his resume. Steve's lackadaisical attitude toward finding a new job made me work that much harder while he just coasted along. Not only did I become resentful of him, I failed to see how I was part of the problem. In doing so much of what he should have been doing for himself, I encouraged his idleness. I also allowed denial to creep in again. Whenever I began to think, "I don't want a guy who lacks ambition," I'd dress up the negative as a positive, "I'm glad Steve isn't materialistic and consumed by getting ahead."

- Are you jumping in to solve the problems of your boy/girlfriend? If so, how?
- What have been the results of your attempts to "rescue" your boy/girlfriend? Have your attempts helped or not? Explain.
- Does your boy/girlfriend have disappointing traits that you're trying to avoid acknowledging?
- Instead of seeing these traits for what they are, do you trick yourself into seeing them only as you want to (e.g., instead of seeing her drinking problem, you tell yourself and

others, "She just likes to have fun"?). If so, list the disappointing trait(s) and how you rationalize it.

What attracted me to Steve was the chance to make an important difference in his life, to do for him what no one else ever had: motivate him to advance in his career and "make something of himself." The fact that he didn't have this desire himself didn't even register with me. As a child, I thought that only I had that "special power" to help my dad, to make him happy when so much about his life made him sad. That was my last memory of him before he left home. With Steve, I picked up these same emotions. I had an exaggerated sense of my own power over his life, resorting to the same typical childlike thinking I'd had as a girl with my dad.

- Do you sometimes feel like you always have to be the strong one in your relationship?
- Are there any ways in which your boy/girlfriend has been strong for you? If so, how?
- Do you respect your boy/girlfriend? If so, in what ways?
- What "unfinished business" might you be working through in your dating relationship?
- Do you honestly feel that you are ready to be involved in a serious relationship?
- In what ways might you need to grow on your own before you truly are ready?

If you find yourself unhappy in your relationship, having serious doubts about whether it's "right" or just not sure if you're ready to be involved, what's the best course of action you can take?

The best gift I gave myself as a young adult was spending a year or so without dating. This hiatus gave me the chance to come to grips with my feelings of having been rejected and deserted by my father. It forced me to go where I most needed and feared to go: accepting that my father wasn't coming back to be the father I needed him to be, and that no one or nothing could *ever* make up for that loss.

I could only do this as a single and unattached person, otherwise the temptation to expect a boyfriend to "fill in" for what was lost was too great. Neither our "significant other" nor our parents are responsible for our happiness and feelings. Only we are.

> While it's tempting to blame someone else for not "being or doing enough," the focus needs to be on fixing our own problems and working on our self-confidence, self-love, and self-identity.

We can look to loved ones to provide support, however, the real work, with all its burdens, remains in our hands.

- Do you tend to blame others for your negative feelings?
- If so, what can you do to help yourself take more responsibility for them?
- What area(s) of your life needs the most attention?
- What attitudes do you need to change?

While time can help heal our wounds, they will never go away completely. We don't "get over" grief; we move through it. Hurt, rejection, and abandonment will periodically replay itself as a tune in our lives. In the vignette, for example, when I asked myself how Eric could do this to me, I was reliving a childhood experience of quietly asking my father this same question. Like a healed bone fracture that aches when the weather turns damp and humid, so will "tunes" from our parents' divorce intensify and fade throughout our lives. The more we become aware of this wound and the incidents that aggravate it, the better able we'll be to keep our feelings in perspective and thereby avoid overreacting and making poor judgments.

Living singly also gave me the time and space I needed to get to know who I really was and grow to love that person. Instead of looking to boyfriends to provide me with a sense of self-worth, I recognized in myself the one person responsible for this job. Our parents' separation or divorce interrupts the process of our discovery of who we are and what we want to do in life, especially if it occurs in our teenage years. Not only do we get distracted by the conflicts and worries of the divorce, we get further sidetracked because our own guilt and shame leads us down a path that isn't true to who we are.

In addition to becoming more emotionally self-reliant, being single encouraged me to find ways to be "happy alone." It fostered my emotional independence and maturity and enabled me to discover new interests. As a result, I found an inner strength that I never experienced in or from my relationships.

- Do you know yourself well enough to know what you want and need in a boy/girlfriend?
- Have you sufficiently clarified your values, beliefs, and personal goals? If not, what are you unsure about?
- What are your biggest strengths and weaknesses?
- What type of partner would best complement them?
- Do you consider yourself to be emotionally strong and self-sufficient?
- In what ways might you still need to grow emotionally?
- Are you able to feel contentment alone, or do you avoid being alone?
- What ways could you find to be happy alone (i.e., reading a book, a creative pursuit, pursuing a hobby of some sort, etc.)?

Why is it so important to develop a solid relationship with yourself before you enter a serious relationship? What's wrong with expecting a serious relationship to help you "come to terms with" the past?

A social psychology professor I had in college once shared with me a very wise insight about relationships. He said, "One plus one is either greater than two or less than two, but never equal to two." If we don't have a healthy sense of loving who we are, we will not be able to form healthy, close relationships with others. Instead, we'll be lured into "codependent" connections, feeding off another and believing we "can't survive" without him or her. This way of relating will never be fulfilling, and such relationships aren't likely to last. Too many (unrealistic) expectations for emotional gratification placed on the shoulders of another will not hone our self-identity.

- Are you looking for your boy/girlfriend to make you feel better about yourself? to give you a sense of identity?
- Do you have an identity apart from your boy/girlfriend? If so, what is it?
- Are you dating someone whom you feel you "couldn't live without"? If so, what is it that you can't live without?
- Review your answer to the previous question. Do any of your needs indicate an over-dependency? If so, how could you take responsibility for meeting those needs on your own?

- In what ways do your needs burden your dating relationship?
- Do you find yourself often becoming clingy or jealous?
- Imagine being in your boy/girlfriend's shoes. Are any of your expectations unfair or unrealistic?
- How does it feel to be on the opposite end of the relationship?

What, then, makes a good relationship work? In her book, *Lucky in Love: The Secrets of Happy Couples and How Their Marriages Thrive*[7], Catherine Johnson claims that, for a marriage to be happy, the partners need to be similar in background (i.e., age, religion, economic status) but different in personality. The shared reference points make marriages work better, while differing personalities allow couples to balance or compensate for each other. I have found this truth borne out in my own marriage as well.

- What do you think makes for a successful, lasting marriage?
- In what ways do you need a boy/girlfriend to complement you?
- What type of personality would provide a good balance for who you are?
- What caused your parents' marriage to fail?
- What have you learned from their situation that you can apply to your own dating relationships?

Being single allowed me to let God enter my life in a very real and personal way. I experienced God more as a friend and constant companion, present to me in everyday, ordinary moments. My inner connectedness to God was the very seed that nurtured my sense and love of myself. This, indeed, is the crucial starting point for any healthy and mature relationship.

---

[7] Catherine Johnson, Ph.D., *Lucky in Love: The Secrets of Happy Couples and How Their Marriages Thrive*, New York, NY; Viking Penguin, 1993.

CHAPTER NINE

Family

Well, Anita took almost all the furniture," Sue's dad says. Sue presses the telephone receiver closer to her ear. It's been four months since she's heard from him.

"My neighbor called this morning to tell me she had moving vans in the driveway. When I got home, everything was gone."

"She took everything?"

"Yup, all except the piano, the treadmill, and the rest of my exercise equipment. But I don't care, she can have it all. She needs the furniture more than I do anyway. Oh, I could still use a lamp here and there, a coffee table, maybe another plant or two. But I have almost everything I need. So, I was thinking, now that things are a bit quieter around here, how about visiting your dear old dad?"

His warm tone surprises Sue, scares her a little. She doesn't know what to say, so she doesn't say anything.

"You don't have to decide right now, but think about it and let me know." He goes on to mention some of the restaurants he'd like to take her to and some of the clothing stores she might like. As he talks, she imagines them walking around the city and talking, just the two of them. She thinks of all the clothes he'd probably buy her and how he'd brag about her to everyone, telling them she is his daughter.

"I know there are a few stores that Anita really liked. I could take you there. One of them has a great selection of jeans. Anita was always buying jeans. She had jean jackets, shirts, vests, hats, purses…you name it. Of course, she looked great in all of it. That was one thing about her; she knew how to take care of herself. Exercised almost every day, watched everything she ate, too."

Sue walks to the window and looks out. She wishes her father would say something about her being pretty.

"Oh, hang on a minute," he says. "I have a beep."

She looks past the next-door neighbor's backyard and toward the gazebo. Its spire pokes toward the sky. She's never heard her dad so distracted like this.

A few more seconds pass, and he comes back on. "Thought that might be Anita, but it was just a telemarketer."

"Dad, are you sure you're OK?"

"I'm fine. I don't want you to be concerned about anything. I have a good job. That's the main thing. I just want to put in a good day every day, then I don't really care what happens the rest of the time."

Sue knows he doesn't mean that. No one can live that way. She imagines him sitting all alone with hardly any furniture, and it hurts her. She begins to realize that he needs her as a mother, not so much as a daughter. This isn't how it's supposed to be, but she knows she has to accept where he is, if she wants a relationship with him at all.

"We start school earlier this year," Sue finally says. "I think it's that last week in August."

"How about visiting sometime this month then, say in two weeks? I'll send you a check, just in case."

"OK," she says. "That should work fine."

They talk for a couple more minutes, then her dad gets a call from one of his business partners and has to go.

Sue hangs up and slouches back on her couch. "God, please help him. Please." She asks God to help her take care of her own needs so she can better help her dad. She looks at the picture of Jesus above her stereo. She stares at his eyes looking up, the trust in them. He was tested so many times, and still he believed, she says to herself. Maybe things have to be difficult sometimes, for everyone, so that you can really learn from them and grow. She thinks of some of the best teachers she's had in school. They were always the ones who gave a ton of homework and had the toughest tests. Maybe it's the same way with God.

*

When my parents separated, I had no idea how my family was supposed to be a family anymore, or if we ever really could be. Even though the separation was a huge relief, it still ripped our lives apart. Rationally, we all knew there was no hope of reconciliation between them—the fighting had gone on for too long and had led to too many problems. We weren't prepared for the changes, however, nor did we discuss them. I have never been able to remember the day my father left, but I have felt the division within myself and my family ever since. It was as if we were a rack of balls in a game of pool, and my dad's departure was the cue ball that made the opening break, scattering us in all directions.

The ways in which we each chose to cope with the separation made my feelings of division even more intense; you may have noticed your brother or sister having completely different feelings and reactions than you do. There are disconnections we may feel when our parents form new dating and marital relationships. If one of your parents made a "significant other" the center of his or her world, you may well have felt so excluded that you felt like little more than a piece of furniture in the room. Or maybe the divorce has made one of your parents so needy that roles are reversing and you feel like you are the parent.

Sue certainly feels that way. She longs for her father to show her exclusive attention and make her feel special. However, he's so consumed by Anita that Sue begins to believe she has to mother him like a child.

> We all heal differently. It is important to respect and accept the individual journeys of other family members in this regard, and to look deeply at what their reactions might be saying about their needs.

Silence is often the best and only response that helps a family member take account for him or herself. Maybe your sister is so angry that she simply needs you to listen without interjecting your opinions and feelings, or perhaps your brother cannot shake his feelings of false guilt and needs you to help him realize that the divorce is not his fault.

It's never easy to see family members caught up in unresolved grief, nor is it easy to realize that we cannot live their journeys or do for them what they need to do for themselves in order to heal. But we still have to do what we can, letting them know we are there for them whenever and however they might choose to turn to us.

- How well are your family members coping with the divorce?
- In what positive or negative ways are they working through their pain?
- Are you and other family members at different stages of healing? If so, explain the differences.
- What do you think your parents and siblings most need to do in order to heal?
- What can you do to help them? What can you *not* do to help them?

I worried constantly about my family after the separation, especially my parents and their emotional survival. Each time I came home from school and found my mother napping on the couch or a letter from my father in the mailbox, I knew the very people I depended on the most were struggling greatly. I was determined to put things back in order in some way. I began to make dinner most nights, cleaned the kitchen, did most of the yard work, and did my best to make straight A's in school while never getting into trouble. I tried to make up for all that was falling apart around me by becoming the "perfect child." Soon thereafter, I stepped into the role of caretaker, especially with my mother. I was petrified of her fading away, like my father had done, so I assigned myself the task of "rescuing" her from her grief. As a young adult, I took on more responsibility by trying to be the "peacemaker" who fixed the problems between family members. Everyone confided in me, arming me with information that I felt impelled to act upon to help them "make amends." Despite my good intentions, however, I ended up putting myself in the middle of heated battles and doing the very work that my family members needed to do themselves.

- How has your parents' divorce changed your role in your family?
- In what specific ways have you had to take on more responsibility?

Sometimes, this added responsibility can be a good influence, helping us to "grow up" and focus on the more important things in life. At other times, though, these added responsibilities end up putting us in a double bind, a seemingly no-win situation in which we don't know where to draw the line. We may feel guilty for dating, or even going out and spending time with friends while Mom or Dad sits at home feeling lonely; or we may feel resentment for not being able to go out with friends because we have to watch a younger brother or sister so that our mom or dad can go out on a date. At such times, it may seem nearly impossible to help our family while taking those steps toward independence that we need to take.

- What conflicts have the increased responsibilities resulting from your parents' divorce caused for you?
- How have you handled these conflicts?
- Did it work?

There are no easy rules for resolving these conflicts. Every family will have different factors fueling their disagreements. There are certain skills, however, that can help us work through them. They don't involve shouting, screaming, threatening, pouting, or any manipulative games, but instead use effective communication. Some approaches that may help you include:

1. **Treating the problem rationally, perhaps even more rationally than your parent(s).**
2. **Anticipating the problem (e.g., asking your parent in advance about finances for college or who'll watch a younger sibling when you both have dates).**
3. **Not attacking or undermining a family member, but honestly expressing your feelings about a situation.**
4. **Letting family members express their feelings, just as you need to express yours.**
5. **Not trying to be "all things to all people," but instead asking for help when you need it.**

I have often hesitated to try to help my family because I feared that sharing in their struggles would overwhelm me too much and just serve to set me back. Besides, how in the world could I reach out to them and maintain a real sense of family, when I was still struggling to help myself?

- What could you do to improve your way of solving problems with your family members?
- Once you nail down better ways to handle the immediate conflicts in your family, what can you do to try and be a "real family" again?
- How can you help one another out, beyond the practicalities of earning extra money, household chores, running errands, and babysitting?
- Is it realistic to hope that you can be a family again when most of your family members are still consumed by grief?

My older brother, Marc, showed me a way. He was fifteen years old when my dad left, a bit wiser than I was at eleven, but still filled with the same questions and too few answers. He would often share his feelings about our parents and the separation while sitting with me underneath the cherry blossom tree in our front yard or whenever we had just finished watching a TV show in the family room. I would be quiet and listen, sometimes sharing thoughts and feelings of my own. I felt safe and protected having my "big brother" there, trying to make sense of all the changes. We both knew we were "in this together," and by experiencing many of the same emotions we were able to understand each other's feelings and concerns and offer reassurance to each other.

Being able to count on Marc when my whole world felt like it was falling apart was one of the greatest comforts I had after our father left. It reassured me that I was not alone and that it was OK to have fears, worries, doubts, and insecurities. This sharing nurtured a special closeness between my brother and me that is unlike any I have witnessed between siblings. It also gave me a positive example for how to relate to the rest of my family in what would become our lifelong journey of healing.

Sue also tried to be there for her father in his time of need. While she would rather have been talking with him about school and her friends, she accepted his need to talk about his problem. She knew he was really hurting, as it wasn't like her father to "unload," and she tried to be there for him by listening, even though she wished the situation was different. She did what she could to reach out to him and maintain a sense of family.

- In what ways are you trying to reach out and maintain a sense of family with your family?
- If you're not doing this, how might you start to do so?
- Who in your family is in greatest need of healing? What can you do (and not do) to help this family member on his or her path?
- With whom in your immediate family or among your relatives might you be able to share freely your feelings about your parents' divorce?
- In what way(s) might this person be able to help you?

Today, when I think of family, I think of the ones whom I am most responsible for helping to the best of my ability. Hand in hand with this obligation is the need to accept them "where they are," with all their weaknesses and failings and in whatever struggle they are experiencing. This may mean being the first to reach out, to forgive, but it is the only response that brings peace and fosters closeness.

- What does family mean to you?
- What are the good aspects of your family?
- How has your family remained a family despite your parents' divorce?
- Has your parents' divorce provided opportunities for you to draw closer to your family? If so, how?
- What added obligations do you see yourself as now having?
- What special role or positive example have you taken on or could you take on?
- In what ways has your family benefited from your parents' divorce?

Extending myself to my family hasn't always been easy, especially when I haven't been met halfway or when family members weren't fulfilling the role that they once did. In these instances, I would often have an attitude of "what have you done for me lately?" Often, it led to hurt feelings, negative judgments, and of distancing myself.

- Consider those family members who are most upsetting to you. What negative attitudes or judgments do you have toward them?
- How have these attitudes or judgments influenced you to act toward them?
- What is it you want from them but are not receiving?

My negative attitudes and judgments never got me anywhere. What they did bring me, instead, was a lot of inner turmoil. It was in those moments that I especially needed to bring God into the relationship.

> Once I turned to God, I found that much of my disappointment resulted from my not knowing what God's plan or purpose was for me in my family relationships.

As I prayed, I gradually discovered that this plan didn't mean having the kind of relationships I had been expecting and hoping for, nor did it mean getting what I was so convinced that I needed. What it did mean was taking a harder path, one that would demand far more from me, yet one that, ultimately, would bring me deeper fulfillment than had life gone "my way."

> Prayer helped me to get past my negative attitudes and judgments and see my family as people who were having difficult struggles.

This freed me to see the truth beyond my immediate reactions. As difficult as these relationships were to accept at times, they provided me with the very opportunities for growing in love by imitating God's love more fully—God who loves us in spite of our weaknesses, who takes us back even after we've sinned, and who waits as long as it takes for us to return to the divine mercy.

- Put any negative attitudes and judgments aside and try to look at these same family members more objectively. What struggles might they be experiencing?
- Consider God, who wants you to be at peace with this person. What purpose might God have for you in this relationship?

Once I became more aware of my family's struggles, another challenge came along. It was the challenge to realize the limits of what I could do for them and leave the rest in God's hands. Experiencing the grief of my family has, at times, cut so deeply that I tried to solve their problems for them. Instead of realizing and accepting that they had to work through their problems at their own rate, I repeatedly tried to get them to "hurry up and heal" by arguing my perspectives or lecturing them about forgiveness. My good intentions have often backfired, however, because I failed to realize what my family members needed most in these moments. They weren't looking for advice or needing to understand forgiveness. They needed me to share in their pain and confusion, to simply be with them in their grief.

Letting my family work through their own struggles has been the most difficult challenge I have faced with them. It has taken me a long time to learn that, but I have finally accepted that no matter how much it hurts to let go, it is something I must do. I simply cannot take their grief away no matter what I do, nor can I help them grow if they don't have this desire themselves.

I have also learned to accept that God does the inviting in these situations as well. When I have tried to invite myself into the struggles of my family members, I have only encountered resistance. I have had to wait for God to open these doors and bring family members to me, wait while praying and trusting that the Holy Spirit was at work in their lives. I have had to accept that this praying and trusting, indeed, can be enough and that letting go doesn't mean abandoning them. Sharing the load is precisely what God asks of us time and again: to be more compassionate and make that first move or turn the other cheek, simply because it is what a family member needs.

Far easier said than done, I realize. I often resist doing so, thinking "Why does it always have to be me?" Yet, in quiet moments, I hear God nudging me to focus on what my family member needs instead of what I feel "entitled to." When I find it difficult to reach out in love, I have to remind myself of my desire to be a good Christian. I know what God expects from me, and if my Christianity doesn't show itself in action, especially in those instances when it is toughest, then it probably isn't doing me much good.

- What are examples of your "doing that little extra" for a family member? What was the result?

- What are your views and feelings about "making the first move" or "turning the other cheek" in your family relationships?

There were times when I took a mental count of what I had done to show love and concern to a family member and compared that to what he or she had done in return. This attitude never led to anything good, however. It prevented me from honoring that higher calling to love and serve as a positive example, and it killed any chance of that family member growing from my "love."

Trying to reach out to my family has not been easy, but I have found that God blesses my efforts. It all started with my intention to try to be loving toward my family and to do something good with my life. Once I committed myself to this, God graced my life with the support of a nurturing boyfriend, a job with flexible hours so I could pursue my career dreams more fully, etc.

- What family member(s) do you find it difficult to love? Explain why.
- What perspective or attitude could you adopt toward this person and your relationship that would help you do a better job of loving him or her?
- What steps are you taking or could you take that would not only encourage your growth, but the growth of your family as well?
- What "helps" do you need God to provide you with along the way?

All your good intentions and efforts notwithstanding, you may still encounter resistance from your family. I have seen a dynamic at work in some families where one member moves on, while the others try to pull him or her back down by resorting to guilt trips or other destructive tactics. Indian village crabs actually exhibit this behavior. When one of them tries to leave the pack, the others pull it back. Just remember that if a family member has a problem with you doing something that's good and loving for yourself, then the real problem resides in that family member. You need to recognize the problem but stay true to your own values, convictions, and goals.

> Don't let the dysfunction of family members become your dysfunction.

We all want a family in which we are loved, accepted, and nurtured for who we are. However, even in the most seemingly "normal" of families that doesn't always happen. We can, however, take solace in the knowledge that God is on our side and remains our true parent no matter what we face.

Many teens of divorce whom I've met over the years have also expressed hurt because their parents were not emotionally present to them during the divorce. The emotional stress your parents feel during and following their divorce may reduce the amount of attention they can give you. In most cases, this is temporary, but sometimes the emotional support you require may still be lacking even years after the divorce happened. There are cases where parents are permanently unavailable emotionally. They will never be there in the ways you need, e.g., to encourage you in your dating relationships or career goals, attend your graduation, or help you financially with college, etc.

> Rather than letting disappointment alienate us from our parents, we need to realize that everyone has limitations and weaknesses, and try to find our support system elsewhere.

It will help you see past your expectations to who your family members really are and, consequently, what they may not be able to give you.

- Do you sometimes look to family members for support and understanding when they can't provide it because of their shortcomings or because of being too burdened with their own struggles?
- If so, who in your family does this pertain to?
- Who in your life supports your steps toward growth?
- What support system is available to you outside of your immediate family (e.g., friends, clubs or sports teams, church support groups or youth groups, etc.)?
- Who serves as a positive example of growth for you?

Another way in which family can hold us back and keep us immersed in its problems is through emotional triangles. Charles L. Whitfield, M.D., a well-respected doctor, psychotherapist, and author of *Boundaries and Relationships,* gives an example:

> If mother and father have a conflict they cannot resolve, one of them may involve the child in such a way that their conflict and pain is transferred to an interaction between the other two...the formed triangle takes away the responsibility that the mother and father could take upon themselves to work through their conflict. This original conflict did not belong to the child.[8]

This situation certainly isn't unique to parents. It could be that you have pressured your parents into a triangle or have witnessed your siblings doing so. This scenario is not unique to families of divorce, either; however, it can be more problematic for us, especially when family members use the triangle to vent unresolved anger at an ex-spouse or parent.

- Does one of your family members repeatedly find fault with another, making you feel as if have to come to the defense of that family member?
- Has a family member ever vented so much about another family member that you feel pressured to side with the person who's venting just to minimize the tension?

I have been involved in family triangles many times, sometimes taking sides in the process. Such a response, however, has only served to divide my family further, with the result of preventing any of us from growing. It is healthier for everyone involved to resist this temptation and stay emotionally neutral. This doesn't imply being uninvolved but trying to help everyone focus on the facts while trying to make sure that all viewpoints are heard. That is the only way we avoid being put in an unfair position and/or avoid jeopardizing other family relationships in the process. Letting the work and

---

[8] Charles L. Whitfield, M.D., *Boundaries and Relationships*, Deerfield Beach, FL: Health Communications, Inc., 1993, p. 160.

pressure for resolving the problem remain between the two "warring" family members is the only way any such tension has a chance of being resolved. What can make these emotional triangles even more difficult to settle are previously unresolved hurts that serve to magnify the present problem.

At other times, a family member can be angry with another even though the bulk of that anger really belongs to someone else in the family. In this scenario, siding with the angry family member may only affirm his or her way of handling the problem and dissuade the need to confront the bigger issue that may lay beneath it.

Taking sides often ends up putting you in the middle of the squabble; when one family member vents to you about a third party, you can easily end up being used as the "messenger." Stay out of the situation, and tell the first to tell the other person himself or herself, thereby leaving the problem and its tension between the two persons involved.

- What are the triangles in your family?
- What can you do to prevent yourself from coming between family members who don't get along or who need to reconcile with one another?
- How do you usually respond to arguments that erupt in your family?
- Does your approach help to resolve problems? If not, what other approach or new ways of relating might work better?

The call to love and to forgive our family members may well be the most difficult challenges of our lives. Giving into feelings of "what we're owed" and letting that set the standard of how we act will never let us have true closeness with members of our family. Nor will it give us that deep sense of pride, joy, and peace that results from approaching life "God's way."

For me, taking personal responsibility to grow in my life through trying to understand what God's plan is has been the only solution that has worked, both in advancing in my own life and in letting go of taking responsibility for all the problems of my family. Making that effort has made personal growth and human maturity possible and life-giving for me.

Notes

CHAPTER TEN

Your Image of God

J ohn and his mom are at Sunday morning Mass. John is wear-
ing a suit jacket and tie, and his mom has on her best blue
dress. They don't want anyone to look at them and think
they're not coping well. They're seated in a pew halfway down the
aisle, neither too close nor too far from the altar—a safe place, where
they're unlikely to be noticed.

The priest steps up to read the gospel. He's six feet tall and has
broad shoulders and a big potbelly. The lectionary sits open on the
ledge directly in front of him. As the priest reads the gospel, John
thinks of God sitting on a throne in heaven with a big white book in
his lap, noting everyone's mistakes with a red marker. John looks
around at the people in church, imagining how long their lists are.
God must see an awful lot of mistakes. It's no wonder God distances
himself from people so easily and sends them to hell. Does anyone
ever get to go straight to heaven?

Finishing the gospel, the priest picks up the book and kisses the
text just read. "Praise to you, Lord Jesus Christ," John says along with
the congregation. They all sit down, and the priest starts the homily.

John's mind continues to drift. He sees God writing "got divorced"
in the big white book, writing it in capital letters so big that it takes
up a whole page. He wonders if God has written up his argument
with Cindy yet and how many spaces it took up. Perhaps God has an
eraser, too, that he uses whenever people go to confession. John isn't
sure, but one thing he does know: he isn't going to ask either of his

parents for advice about his relationship. They're probably still on God's "hell list."

Living through our parents' divorce can put us on a collision course with God, a point from which we either let our disappointment challenge us to know God more deeply, or from which we distance ourselves, maybe never giving God a real chance again.

Maybe you're wondering why you should even consider inviting God into your struggle. After all, you're doing OK right now. The question is, however, are you at peace and satisfied? In my own case, my feelings and emotions were so heavy and negative that I realized I needed some kind of life-affirming context to channel them toward. I needed to draw on a strength outside of myself if I was ever to experience any peace or any satisfaction. I needed the help of Jesus.

The question for us here is: How we can let our difficulties take us closer to God? What does it take for us to build a positive relationship with God, so that our parents' divorce can become a source—an opportunity—for personal growth?

To answer these questions, we need to examine our image of God to see if we are locked in misconceptions or negative feelings we may have about the divine.

- What are your attitudes about God right now?
- What would you most like to say to God right now regarding your parents and/or their divorce? (Write down all that comes to mind.)
- Do you expect God to step in and make the unfairness of your situation right again?
- Do you believe that God cannot do this and still love you? (Journal your answers, and see what it tells you about your views and attitudes toward God.)
- Do you sometimes point your finger at God for the wrongs you experience as a result of your parents' divorce? If so, what wrongs do you blame God for?
- Are you expecting God to step in and make the unfairness of your situation right again?[9]

---

[9] In Chapter 7, "Rejection by God," we explored this subject more fully.

My image of God has changed over the years, pretty much as a reflection of my changing attitudes and feelings toward my father. When I was a young girl, I thought of God much like I did Santa Claus or a teacher in school who would reward good behavior and punish bad. This was precisely the way in which I first related to my father. He was a good provider who enabled my family to live in a beautiful ranch house in an upper middle-class neighborhood. Because of him, I was able to get new clothes each school year, take piano and dance lessons, and go swimming at a country club. I saw God as I did my dad, as the bearer of gifts and as someone whom I asked to do what I wanted.

After my dad left home, and the years passed without his return, I was haunted by questions that I had no answers for. Little about my relationship with my dad made sense, and I started to question his love for me. I transferred this uncertainty and distrust onto God, concluding that God couldn't see anything good in me either and that God's love probably wasn't real. I still went to church each Sunday and holy day, but deep down my lack of trust led me to distance myself from God more and more. God began to seem more like a prosecuting attorney, always looking to find fault with who I was and what I did.

In the vignette, John also has a negative, unloving image of God. His God was a very judgmental God who constantly focused on everyone's mistakes. This image prevented John from praying in church, because he was too busy thinking about everyone else's mistakes. Finding plenty of fault in his parents, like he imagined God did, he adopted a judgmental attitude that caused him to distance himself both from God and his parents.

- How would you describe the God you relate to?
- Is it similar to any other relationships in your life? If so, which ones?
- How does your image of God influence your attitude toward others? The way you treat others?

My image of God eventually changed in a positive way in my young adult years. I wasn't getting anywhere on my own and finally decided to take a risk and "give God another chance" to help me. Gradually, I learned to "let go and let God," opening myself more and more to what God's way might be. The faith of my childhood deepened and matured to where I began to ask what God wanted *me* to do, rather than focusing on what I thought *God* should do.

As I learned to rely more on God to help me, I gained what can best be described as a loving friend and abiding Spirit. At first, this wasn't something I was conscious of; it was something that grew out of my prayer life. This is how I relate to God still today.

As a loving friend, God comforts and nurtures me, someone who is always beside me, wanting the best for me. This lets me know that God knows me and my deepest needs better than I know them myself. This love is intense, far greater than I or anyone else can fathom. This love gives me great comfort and confidence, letting me know God is there for me always and ready to help, no matter what the situation or the hour.

As abiding Spirit, God repeatedly guides me in subtle ways. At times, this feels like someone tapping me on the shoulder, urging me to pay extra attention to a person or situation. This tapping can even come from what someone says during an interview on a radio news show, a comment that—while made in a different context—gives me insight into a family member I'm at odds with. At other times, the Spirit whispers to me when I'm driving in the car (with the radio off) and warns me against doing the wrong thing.

Through this influence of the Holy Spirit, I've come to discover more and more of God's plan for me. Growing up, I experienced the Holy Spirit through the nagging desire I had to understand who my father really was, despite the negative remarks I often heard about his character and love for me. The Spirit instilled in me this extra motivation; it was a life-affirming influence that helped me try harder.

- What person loves you the most?
- Describe the loving aspects of your relationship with this person.
- Could (or does) your relationship with God have these same characteristics? If not, why not?
- Do you have a question or concern about your parents that always seems to be nagging at you? If so, what is it and how are you trying to resolve it?
- Is it working, or do you need to rely more on God's help?

God's essence and true being is, of course, beyond any human images or concepts. This "beyond-ness," however, doesn't take away our need and ability to experience a positive, loving image of God. We gain it by opening ourselves to trust the guidance of the Spirit, and we need it to acquire the strength and direction required for healing.

Scripture provides us with many good images for God. In the Book of Genesis, God is seen as creator, and in the Book of Exodus as liberator, freeing the Israelites from slavery in Egypt.

If you find it difficult to sense how God relates to you in a personal way, it may be helpful to think of a symbol that describes God's nearness to you. The symbol of a long winding path through nature is an image that helps me connect and "see" God as part of the journey I'm called to travel. This path has both peaks and valleys, safe clearings and beautiful rainbows, peaceful streams and cold, dark woods, scratchy weeds and slippery rocks that, at times, make it difficult for me to find my way.

- What symbols come to mind when you think of who God is?
- What specifically about this symbol describes God for you?

I have also come to know God as a consuming fire that works to burn away the weaknesses, doubts, and distractions that take me away from Jesus. God's hand works through every aspect of my life in ways that are always best for me, even when denying me "things" (e.g., my father's return) and using my hurts to make me aware of where God's beckoning directs me and encourages my growth.

- Consider your parents. What is the greatest weakness, doubt, or negative feeling you have that keeps you distanced from them?
- If you let God help burn this obstacle away, how could your relationships with your parents change? Note some of the possibilities.
- How might God be calling you in your relationship with your mom and dad?
- What special gifts in yourself can you draw on to grow closer to your parents?

- What risks could you take that might lead you on a better path with them?

Another way in which we might come to know God is through attention to a certain kind of "force" or "energy" in our lives. This may have much to do with how we experience our parents' influence. I often experience God as strengthening, empowering, and encouraging me to grow and act. At times, this has meant taking risks in a relationship or going after career opportunities that would stretch my abilities. As scary as that was, I felt that God was giving me the grace that confirmed I was on the right path. My mother has had this same influence in my life, urging me to "do the right thing" as well as that "little extra" to show kindness toward others. As a result, I often see God influencing me to serve others.

God has also been present to me in a calm, patient way similar to my father's influence in my life. My father has always been a voice of wisdom, giving me perspective and an outlook to reflect upon. I find God speaking to me in the same way, encouraging me to look and listen intently to the important things that happen around me. I need to wait patiently for this wisdom, and while at times it presents itself clearly and unexpectedly, it always requires me to listen and be receptive.

- How would you describe the primary positive influence or "force" your father has had in your life?
- How would you describe the primary positive influence or "force" your mother has had in your life?
- Do you perceive God as influencing you in these same ways? If so, describe an incident.

Once we have a positive context for growing in our understanding of God, we begin to recognize that we are on a spiritual journey. This positive perception is what we need to cling to, time and again, as we work through our negative feelings. Inviting God into our struggles will both help us to heal and see a deeper purpose and meaning in them. No longer will we be consumed and controlled by the uncontrollable; instead, we'll find a much needed balance that frees us and allows us to accept these negative circumstances as "teachable moments" which help us grow closer to God.

CHAPTER ELEVEN

Surrendering to God

I'm lying on the bottom bunk bed in my dorm room, unable to say my prayers like I usually do. I feel like such a fool for, once again, having asked God to bring Dad and me closer. Every time I do, our relationship only gets worse.

"This is all wrong, God," I finally say.

I roll over, scrunch the pillow underneath my head. I've tried so hard, and things just keep getting worse. Maybe I'm whimping out. Then again, I have no clue what to do, anyway.

In the hallway, shouts of laughter sound, then footsteps patter down the stairs.

It gets quiet again.

I roll on my back. The lamppost in the quad shines through the blinds, lighting the crucifix that stands on my middle bookshelf. I know Jesus is here with me, but I don't want to talk to him. All I can think about is how he could make things a whole lot easier for me if only he wanted to.

Deep down, I know Jesus loves me, even though so many things about Dad make no sense. I remain quiet, thinking of Jesus being there. I begin to realize all the things I cannot control, like whether or not a guy will fall in love with me and if Mom will be OK by herself if I move away after graduation.

It's the same way with Dad. I can't make him call or write. I can't make him do anything.

An airplane flies over our building.

I continue listening.

This problem with Dad will never go away. Or be made right.

Tears roll down my face. I feel my insides give way. I begin to realize that it doesn't matter what I want and need from Dad; what matters is getting past that need and moving on.

More tears roll down my face. I let myself feel the hurt. Somehow I know I'm going to be OK.

Surrendering to God poses the greatest challenge for any of us on the journey of healing. As a child, I turned readily and unquestioningly to God, but as I got older, and the years passed without my father's return, I let myself lose my trust in God. I distanced myself, and relied more and more on myself. I convinced myself that the only way my world would not fall apart completely was through my taking as much control of it as possible.

Having our sense of security shaken by the very people we feel totally dependent on encourages us to become very self-protective. I learned pretty quickly to guard my feelings. I became a loner, keeping most people, as well as God, at a distance. That way, I could never be let down by anyone again.

- Has your parents' divorce encouraged you to be gun-shy in your relationships?
- Have you ever vowed never to "let yourself get hurt again"?
- If so, has this vow prevented you from receiving the "nourishment" you need to feel satisfied?
- How has your parents' divorce changed your personality?
- Have you found yourself becoming more withdrawn and isolated from others, more or less aggressive about attaining your goals, more pessimistic, etc.?
- Has the divorce changed your relationship with God as well? If so, how? (For example, have you stopped praying and/or going to Mass? Or are you trying to learn more about God by reading books, etc.?)
- Is God often the last "person" you turn to, if at all, in your struggles?
- If "yes," when faced with a difficult decision, a big fear, worry, or sadness, whom or what do you turn to for comfort?

- Is the comfort you receive lasting or temporary?
- If "no," how do you include God in your struggles?

Part of me wanted to entrust my problems to God, but a bigger part was too afraid. So, I didn't reach out to God, nor did I take chances in any other areas of my life. My entire life became "safe" but frozen. I got no further in finding my career niche, and I remained stuck in dead-end dating relationships. I had convinced myself it was easier not to take the risks necessary to improve my life. Of course, that also meant that I "went nowhere," and I remained dissatisfied.

> Even when we reach out to God and seem to get no answers or improvements in our life, we still need to be open and trust that God has a good reason for things being so.

In the vignette, I was disappointed in God; not only was my relationship with my father not improving, it seemed to be getting worse. Clinging to those feelings and conclusions meant putting up a wall between God and me. I eventually took a chance, however, and insisted on believing that Jesus was there for me.

- Are you satisfied and at peace with where your life is going? If not, what is causing you the greatest difficulty?
- Do you think that you alone have the ability to grow past your dilemmas? Why or why not?
- What has your life shown you so far?
- Consider asking God to help you with your greatest challenges.
- What's the worst that can happen if you give your difficulty over to God? What might you gain from it?

It took a lot of courage and humility for me to finally decide to let God be God. It is not easy to admit to yourself that you don't always know the answers to life. Even though I knew enough to make decent grades in school, I wasn't able to conquer my most difficult challenges on my own.

> Precisely in those moments when we feel overwhelmed by our own inadequacy is our faith truly born.

I was humbled enough to realize that there were some battles I simply couldn't win on my own, no matter how hard I tried. I needed help, a strength outside myself. I needed God.

You may find that the feelings or situations you fear confronting the most are the very ones that can most fully help you discover God's presence and call. This doesn't mean that God deliberately puts you in fear; it means that this is where we are more likely to hear God's voice as a "wake-up call" that stirs us, in some way, to realize this presence and answer the call.[10]

In the vignette, I felt powerless to improve my relationship with my dad. Nothing I did seemed to help. Looking back, I see that I didn't know what was best, only God did. Once I humbled myself to that reality, I discovered what would improve my life and, in turn, improve my relationship with my father.

Our trust and faith in God will be tested from time to time as we journey forward in our understanding and fulfillment of God's plan. Obstacles will come our way, but if we encounter them with faith, we'll catch a glimpse of our dependence on God and the blessing of its beckoning surrender.

- What qualities in your personality hinder you from letting God be God?
- What obstacles are you encountering in trying to follow God's plan (e.g., stepparents, limited exclusive time with your parent, etc.)?
- What unexpected "helps" has God given you that may shed light on God's plan for you with regard to your family?
- What people or groups in your school, church or community are there to support you as you strive to understand and follow God's plan?

---

[10] In Chapter 7, "Rejection by God," I explore a crisis point when God's grace entered my life.

Surrendering to God enabled me to love my family members better. It led me beyond my own hurt to see who they really were. My tendency to take personally what they did and didn't do, which led me to reach faulty conclusions about their feelings toward me, gave way to seeing them in a new, truer light once I realized that their actions reflected their weaknesses and struggles and not a lack of love for me. Surrendering my negative feelings to God was the only way I was able to move past them and thereby grow in wisdom and compassion. It enabled me to have, not the family relationships I had always dreamed of, but the ones God intended for me.

- Do you sometimes feel as though your parents really don't care much about you?
- Could there be another, more accurate reason to explain their behaviors, one on which God could shed more light?

It's important to realize that surrendering is part of growing and healing. It doesn't cause us to become "hapless victims" in any way; quite the contrary, it is a step toward transforming injury and powerlessness into gentle strength in our respective situations.

> Surrendering makes room for a greater power to work in our lives and help us carry our burdens.

Surrendering to God doesn't mean we're required to perform huge "pious" works of holiness every day. It involves an opening of our hearts and minds in a sustained effort to listen to God's voice in us. We can start with a formal prayer, or we can simply talk and listen to God as we would with our best friend, knowing we can be our real selves and still be accepted.

In the vignette, I recognized that Jesus was there for me. I let myself feel his love, and in that moment of trust I was given what I needed to grow and move on. My disappointment about my relationship with my father was still real, but God reached out to help me work through it.

- How might you begin to reach out more to God?
- When could you set aside time on a regular basis to have real talks with God?

I often have the most heartfelt conversations with God when I'm driving alone in my car, as if God were sitting beside me in the passenger seat. I always include time to be silent and listen. Often, God "talks back" to me, giving me a new insight or suggestion that helps me resolve a dilemma.

Reading Scripture also helps me to hear God's voice. As I reflect on God's word, I have often found a certain passage or verse "jump out" at me, as if God was using it to direct and assure me of what to do.

Sometimes, at night, when I find myself unable to sleep because of a worry or fear, I go to my desk where I have a picture of the Sacred Heart of Jesus. I turn on a dim light, sit down, and look into Jesus' eyes. I talk with him as a friend, letting myself surrender to the trust that he listens and cares. Sometimes, without even asking for help, I start to feel more at peace, and gain confidence in my ability to "weather the storm." At other times, all I can do is just sit there in trust, resting my head in my hands, and let him see my weary face. Occasionally, I write down specific requests on slips of paper, such as: "Please help me not feel so responsible for Mom's life. Help me rid my false guilt so I can do your will." Then I fold up the piece of paper and put it behind the picture of the Sacred Heart. It's my way of turning over my most pressing difficulties to Jesus. Weeks or months later, I've opened an old slip and discovered that the problem has been resolved, often without my taking note of it. In placing the stones of my fears and worries in Jesus' hands, he's given them back to me as diamonds of peace.

- Do you have a private, quiet place where you can go and be with God? If so, where? If not, where could you make one?
- Is there a picture or a quote you could take with you as a reminder that God is there?
- What are you having difficulty letting go of? Consider writing these things on slips of paper and placing them in a secret place that "only God knows."

Surrendering to God is an ongoing process. It is what enables us to give back something better than what we've been given. Once we accept and understand suffering, we can transcend it and, like Jesus, move to a place of lasting comfort and peace.

Instead of working so hard to control everything in my life, I have gradually acknowledged what I cannot control. I leave it in God's hands. My task has become one of surrendering and listening for God's voice, and then acting on it. I have begun to see God's hand in every facet of my life.

> The wounds of our parents' divorce will always remain a part of us, an imprint on our souls, but if we learn to surrender those wounds to God, our negative experiences will be transformed into positive, growth-filled ones.

The challenge lies not in denying the hurt but in surrendering to it. With Jesus by our side, we have the grace to move through it by letting it transform us into someone better than we were before. In so doing, we will see how God works through everyday graced moments, in the disappointments as well as the joys.

Remember that Jesus understands our suffering. He has been where we are, and he triumphed over it through his repeated surrender to God's will even in his darkest moments of pain and suffering. If we want to get past our darkness, we must trust in God even when it's most difficult. If we do, God will work through us and for us.

Notes

CHAPTER TWELVE

Forgiveness

Dad and I are on the freeway. We've just finished dinner and are heading back to his house. "Dad," I say, "I just want you to know I'm sorry for everything that's happened. With Mom. And you having to leave. It's been hard for me, but I know it's been hard for you too."

He lowers the volume of the classical piano music. "Well, they say that in every life some rain must fall, so I guess we all have our problems. Deep down, I hurt a lot, because when you needed me, I wasn't there, and I can't forget that. Looking back, I'm not sure what I could have done differently. I just hope that someday I'll see you happy despite my failings."

Glancing over at him, I know that he's sorry in his heart. I can feel that he hurts, like I hurt, alone, inside himself. I don't know how he has been able to handle his guilt.

"It's great to see you, Dad," I finally say. My lips quiver as I smile.

"I'm certainly proud of the fine young lady you've become. I don't know how you've done it. I certainly don't take any credit for it."

"You've instilled a lot of good things in me."

"We do have some things in common, I guess. We're both stubborn, that's for sure." He looks at me and smiles. "But I'd like to think we're both rather smart and deep too."

He turns into the driveway, then pushes the garage door opener. "My main concern was to see that you got a good education. I've tried to make decisions with that goal in mind." He pulls the car into

95

the garage, turns off the engine, and looks down at the steering wheel. "In my own way, I've done my best. I've made my mistakes, but not intentionally. I never wanted to hurt anybody."

My eyes fill with tears as he's talking to me, but I don't hold them back. I feel the weight of his guilt and regrets, and wish I could lift them off of him forever.

He looks slowly toward me. "I love you, Dad." I reach over and hug him. I hold him tight, crying harder as the tears fall down my face. I realize that I really, finally, do.

Most of us would want to forgive our parents, ourselves, or whomever we hold responsible for our parents' divorce and any of the problems we're having because of it. Maybe you wish you could forgive your parents, but you just can't take that first step because you still have too much hurt inside of you. Or maybe you're afraid to forgive because you think it means you'll only get hurt again.

Many people confuse forgiving with forgetting, others do not realize the benefits forgiving someone can bring them.

Are you ready to forgive? Do you know what it involves? No easy shortcut exists on the path to forgiveness. It is one of the most difficult acts that we're ever called to do. Yet it remains the only way we can truly move past our hurts.

- For what do you need to forgive your dad regarding the divorce?
- For what do you need to forgive your mom regarding the divorce?
- Make a list of these items, and put a star beside those that you find it hardest to forgive them for.
- What difficulties in particular do you blame your parents for?
- Are you holding on to a desire to "get even" with them?
- When you think about them or are around them, do you automatically find yourself focusing on their mistakes and what they haven't done right in your life?

I needed to forgive my parents for many things. I needed to forgive my dad for not being at my piano recitals and my high school graduation, and the way his absence caused me to feel so self-conscious and insecure. I needed to forgive him for not being there to see my report cards, to approve of my boyfriends, and for not saying "I love you" when I needed to hear those words. I needed to forgive my mom for getting married too young instead of waiting until she was more mature and independent and therefore better prepared for such a serious commitment. I had to forgive both my parents for not finding a way, other than bitter fighting, to resolve their problems.

Whenever a friend at school hurt me, my mother's response was always the same: "Show that you're the bigger person." While this advice helped me keep many friendships, I fought it every step of the way when it came to my parents. "Why does it have to be me?" I'd think. "They should be the ones who should be trying to make up for how dumb and irresponsible they've been; after all, they're the adults." The fact that my parents had made a mistake, gotten divorced, and brought all kinds of problems into my life because of it, was already unfair enough in my mind. Expecting me now to "be the bigger person" and forgive was, for a long time, more than I could handle.

> Forgiving others, especially parents, is risky business. It feels safer to hold on to the anger, disappointment, and justified resentment.

Withholding forgiveness may also convince us that they can't hurt us again. However, whom do we ultimately hurt the most by not forgiving?

- Do you sometimes feel as though you'll only get hurt again if you truly forgive your parents?
- Is there any other bad outcome you fear might happen if you forgive them?
- Do you think your parents "deserve" to be forgiven? Why or why not?

In my mid-twenties, I remember feeling a recurring sadness for a long time, even though I had no obvious reason to be sad. I was living on my own and supporting myself; I had a decent car and job; I was dating and in good health. However, one area of my life remained at a dead-end: my relationship with my parents. I had built up walls with them, and it was tearing me up inside. I finally reached the point where I said to myself, "This is wrong and unfair. It will always be wrong and unfair. But I'm not going to let it ruin my life. I have to find a way to start over with them."

Forgiving doesn't mean forgetting. We're not expected to, nor should we, forget the hurt done to us. God wants us to be careful in our relationships. The real issue we need to focus on is whether or not we should entrust ourselves to the person who hurt us. In other words, is this person someone you can depend on, someone who takes responsibility for the effect his or her words and actions have on you?

- What are your attitudes about forgiveness?
- Do you believe forgiveness has the potential to take away your negative feelings and make your relationships better?
- Do you think forgiving someone shows weakness? Please explain.
- Should you entrust yourself to the person who has hurt you? Why or why not?

Forgiving doesn't mean honoring someone who's dishonorable, either. Such action would excuse the bad behavior, which is not what forgiving asks of us. How, then, can we forgive a dishonorable person, especially if he or she doesn't seem to be sorry? The focus or the calling in this situation is to be honorable (e.g., being a better parent yourself), despite the dishonorable example you've been given.

- Has the person you need to forgive shown him or herself to be dishonorable?
- How can you be honorable despite their bad example?
- What has it taught you?

It took me a long time, but I finally reached the point where living my life with contentment and inner peace became more important to me than "playing it safe" by holding on to my hurt. A big part of the struggle, for me, in moving toward forgiveness involved letting go of my expectations. This wasn't because I didn't deserve better, but because it was necessary in order to "move past myself" and acquire the understanding I needed.

This letting go was what enabled me, in the vignette, to realize how much my father was struggling because of the divorce. In so doing, I freed myself from seeing his actions through the filter of my hurt. The only way I would come to the real truth was through seeing his actions as stemming from who he was as a person.

- What hurts and needs are preventing you from understanding better those who have hurt you?
- What do you need to understand about them in order to forgive them more fully?

Understanding who my parents really were, and getting to know them as people rather than as just "Mom and Dad," went a long way in helping me to forgive them. Sometimes I found us speaking completely different languages, even though we were all speaking English. We may expect our parents to "know better," especially when we know ourselves. However, when we step into their shoes and see the world through their eyes, we may find they lack the knowledge, the language, or the ability to speak the words.

Gaining more understanding is only part of the battle, however. It didn't prevent me from judging my parents, from concluding that I was "better" and would never make those same mistakes when I married and had kids of my own. To get past this judgmental attitude, I needed to make a real commitment to forgiving them. This meant forgiving not just whenever I felt like it, or whenever it suited me; it meant forgiving them each and every time any negative thoughts and feelings presented themselves. If I didn't do so, but let this negativity win out, I would only be pushing them farther out of my life, thereby truly jeopardizing any chances for reconciliation.

To forgive them also required a habit of deliberately focusing on my parents' good qualities and the good they had done for me and others. I had to open my heart enough so that I could see them as the good people they are, people who are trying as best they know how.

- What good qualities do your parents have?
- Do you believe that people who hurt others do so because deep down they want to?
- What was your parents' relationships like with their parents?
- If these relationships were problematic or nonexistent, how might that example be influencing your parent's treatment of you?

- What are you doing that might be preventing a reconciliation with your parent(s)?

I began to realize that forgiveness was the only way forward. Even if my parents rejected my attempts, I would have the satisfaction of knowing I had done all I could to improve my relationships with them. This was far better than being locked up in hurt and anger, with heart hardened, and wondering "what if?" for the rest of my life. Most of us have heard much about why we *should* forgive. However, have you ever considered why you might *want* to forgive?

> Forgiving my parents had a ripple effect in my life, both in my relationships with them and with others.

To forgive them enabled me to approach each of them with an open and accepting attitude. This encouraged them to reveal more of their feelings and who they were to me, all of which fostered a general atmosphere of reconciliation between us. Bit by bit, this enabled me to experience the emotional closeness I had been wanting for so long. It also enabled me to forgive others more readily, and it drew others to me because I had a more positive, hope-filled outlook on life. I also noticed a distinct change in my feelings toward other father-daughter relationships. Prior to forgiving my father, I would look jealously, even resentfully, at other girls who had loving relationships with their fathers, feeling as though I had been "cheated." The affectionate gaze and smiles of these fathers toward their daughters always sent a piercing jab into my heart. Later, when guys I dated fussed over their nieces, this also made me feel jealous. I feared having a daughter of my own one day and resenting her closeness with my husband. As I let forgiveness characterize my relationship with my father, though, and our relationship grew, this jealousy washed away.

Failure or refusal to forgive also jeopardizes our relationship with God. Consider the pledge we make in the Lord's prayer: "Forgive us our trespasses as we forgive those who trespass against us." What marks our lives as Christians is precisely this openness to forgive faults and injuries. We need to do so even if our efforts get thrown back in our face. Furthermore, if we want God to forgive us, we must first forgive others from the heart.

- How might forgiving your parents benefit you personally?
- What are the good things that could result from it?

Consider a time when you hurt a friend and later regretted it.

1. **What did this incident show you about your weaknesses and limitations?**
2. **How did this person respond to you afterwards?**
3. **How did it make you feel?**
4. **If this person forgave you, what effect did it have on your relationship with him or her?**
5. **What did this experience teach you about how you appreciate being treated when you've made a mistake and hurt someone?**

If you still find yourself reluctant to forgive the person who's hurt you, consider the harm of not forgiving. What happens to us emotionally and spiritually? We hold on to justifiable resentment that kills our spirit and drains our energies. We may also become so consumed by hurt and anger that we recreate the past, making the same mistakes as the person who hurt us.

What if the parent you need to forgive doesn't admit his or her failings, guilt, or remorse? How can you forgive someone who doesn't seem to be sorry for what he or she has done? Perhaps you haven't seen your dad or mom since he or she left home, and maybe you have no idea where he or she even lives. How are you supposed to forgive someone who completely abandons you?

Let's consider the first circumstance. How do you know your parent isn't sorry? Maybe he or she just doesn't know how to admit it, or is too scared or ashamed to, just as you might be too reluctant or unwilling to admit certain feelings to them. Maybe they're not expressive, in general, when it comes to feelings. As a result, your parent may need you to make that first step by communicating that you love and accept them despite the past.

That's what happened between my dad and me. When I held resentment, anger, and disappointment in my heart, he sensed it and remained at a distance. But when I finally shelved those feelings and met him with openness and acceptance, he admitted his regret and, in his own way, asked for more of my forgiveness.

If abandoned by your parent, you may likely be hurt so deeply you doubt you'll ever be able to forgive him or her. In this matter, what might help is asking God to forgive this parent through you. This can help you open yourself some without having to take an entire step. You may find that it allows God just enough room to heal and strengthen your heart so your forgiveness may continue.

No matter what your situation is, you will find it helpful to write a forgiveness letter to that specific person. You don't mail this letter. It's intended, instead, to help you focus on what you specifically need to forgive this person for.

- Write a forgiveness letter.
- Start by expressing your real feelings about the person who has hurt you and what he or she has done.
- Next, write the words, "But I forgive you," and continue writing, applying your forgiving attitude to the person and situation.
- Repeat this journaling exercise until your feelings are exhausted.

Forgiving others is never easy, mainly because it's such a selfless action. It goes against our fallen human nature. Yet it remains the only way in which we can grow spiritually. As I delved more deeply into forgiving my parents, I felt more and more connected to Jesus' experience on the cross. In reading the New Testament accounts of his last days in Jerusalem, I found the ultimate role model for showing what it means to forgive and, essentially, love others. I learned the humility of identifying with him.

Forgiving my parents and showing this by assuming a more loving and accepting attitude toward them changed my relationships with them dramatically. The most noticeable change was that both my mother and father opened up more to me. I got to know them in ways I never had before—as friends—and I shared a brand new closeness with them as a result. I knew I had affected this change and I felt good about it. It wasn't easy, and it took courage I didn't know I had, but it was one of the most important accomplishments of my life, one that glued my heavy, shattered heart back together and filled it with the light and love I had been searching for all along.

CHAPTER THIRTEEN

Catholic Church Teachings on Marriage and Divorce

Marriage is one of the seven sacraments of the Catholic Church. This means that Catholics believe marriage is not only a celebration, but also a unique meeting with Jesus Christ in which a human union is blessed with the promise of his being with us always. Married Catholics, therefore, find the risen Christ present in their love for each other. As they share their love and lives together, in the context of children and/or the community, they become a symbol, or outward sign, of grace. In this way, marriage serves as God's self-gift of love, given not only for husband and wife, their mutual well-being, and the procreation and nurture of children, but also for the Church and the world at large. The Church teaches that marriage is a personal covenant like that between God and God's people and between Christ and his body, the Church.

The Catholic understanding of marriage is that, when properly entered into, it is a lifelong covenant that only the death of one of the spouses can dissolve. The biblical basis for this is Matthew 19:6: "So they are no longer two, but one flesh. Therefore what God has joined together, let no one separate." *The Modern Catholic Encyclopedia* states:

In the Church's view, all marriages have this essential character of permanence, both those which are "natural" (where one or both persons are not baptized) and those which are sacramental (between two baptized Christians). Because of this deeply held conviction about the indissolubility of marriage, the Church does not recognize that civil divorce terminates the marriage covenant.[11]

The Church views divorce as a deep wound to the natural moral law. "The natural law expresses the original moral sense which enables [human beings] to discern by reason the good and the evil, the truth, and the lie" (*Catechism of the Catholic Church*,1954). It has the force of law because it is the voice and interpreter of a higher reason to which our spirit and our freedom must be submitted.

Unfortunately, however, marriages fail for various reasons, and civil divorce may be the only answer. Getting divorced doesn't make your parents "bad" persons or "bad" Catholics, nor does it imply that they are immoral. The Catechism explains:

> If civil divorce remains the only possible way of ensuring certain legal rights, the care of the children, or the protection of inheritance, it can be tolerated and does not constitute a moral offense.[12]

The Modern Catholic Encyclopedia further notes:

> There are situations, e.g., physical abuse of spouse or children, flagrant adultery, or failure of child support, etc., in which divorce may be morally justified, either as a practical necessity or as the lesser of two evils. In other words, to sue for divorce may or may not be sinful, depending on the circumstances, and to live as a divorced person does not imply a state of sin.[13]

---

[11] *The Modern Catholic Encyclopedia*, Collegeville, MN: The Liturgical Press, 1994, p. 243.
[12] CCC, 238
[13] *The Modern Catholic Encyclopedia*, Op. cit., p. 244.

The Church also recognizes that there are innocent victims in divorce. The Catechism states:

> It can happen that one of the spouses is the innocent victim of a divorce decreed by civil law; this spouse therefore has not contravened the moral law. There is a considerable difference between a spouse who has sincerely tried to be faithful to the Sacrament of Marriage and is unjustly abandoned, and one who through his own grave fault destroys a canonically valid marriage.[14]

Perhaps your parents have wondered if the Church will still accept them now that they are divorced. For example, if your parents are Catholics, can they still receive the sacraments? A divorced Catholic may, when properly disposed, continue to receive the sacraments of Eucharist, penance, and anointing of the sick, and otherwise function fully in the Church. However, the Church says that those who divorce and remarry without obtaining an annulment cannot receive the Eucharist. This is because the Church views remarriage without an annulment as contradicting the union of love between Christ and the Church as well as the Church's teaching about the indissolubility of marriage. For these reasons, such a remarriage is considered morally wrong.

The most common way for a divorced person to marry in the Church (while the former spouse is still living) is to obtain an annulment from a diocesan marriage tribunal. An annulment is a formal declaration by a diocesan tribunal system that the marriage (be it natural or sacramental) was null and void from the beginning. This means that the Church does not recognize the union as valid and sacramental.

Through the annulment process, the Church reflects upon documents presented by petitioners and examination of testimony given by those who know the couple, trying to look into the hearts and minds of the persons as they got married. The tribunal may be able to issue a declaration that what appeared to be a marriage was, in fact, lacking some of the essential elements which must be present. At this point, the marriage may be proclaimed never to have existed in the

---

[14] CCC, 2386

sacramental sense. In other words, it never was a true bond between wife, husband, and God. Consent of the parties is also deemed to have never been legitimately exchanged.[15]

A very important point to remember in all this is that you are not considered "illegitimate" in any way, should one of your parents receive an annulment (can.1137). Nor does the Church's annulment mean that a significant relationship, even a marriage, never existed between your parents. *The Modern Catholic Encyclopedia* explains:

> The marriage relationship had as much real history, human meaning and moral obligation as the partners invested in it....The Church's annulment simply says that, from the point of view of the Church's canon law, the marriage which appeared to be genuine, was originally defective in some way, and that the Church will not take official cognizance of it as an authentic union.[16]

This is so because the Church presumes that your parents married in good faith, even if that is later declared null. An annulment also does not affix blame to either party.

What might be reinforced for you from the Church's teaching as you consider getting married someday yourself? Perhaps your parents' divorce has made you especially gun-shy in this regard. You may even fear repeating your parents' marital mistakes so much that you doubt if you'll ever get married. Do not lose heart or get down on yourself, but let your parents' divorce motivate you to regard that much more seriously the sacrament of matrimony, your intended spouse, and your own readiness for marriage.

Church leaders are placing more emphasis on preparing young adults well for marriage. Readiness for marriage is the crucial starting point to focus on, i.e., making sure that, if marriage is your vocation, you enter into the union and celebrate the sacrament fully capable of giving such a gift and honoring a full and knowledgeable commitment. It is only in this way that the sacrament can be honored as the lifelong covenant it's intended to be.

---

[15] For more on this, see: Fr. William E. Young, Jr., *The What, Why, and How of Marriage Annulments*, Liguori Publications, 2002.

[16] *The Modern Catholic Encyclopedia*, op. cit., p. 31.

Like me, you have probably thought about all the reasons why your parents' marriage didn't work out. You've likely heard stories about why other marriages failed as well, such as the woman becoming pregnant or one or both parties trying to escape a bad home situation. A big reason why these marriage situations fail is because either one or both parties did not make a true choice of marriage for what it is and is meant to do, namely to build a community of life and love.

When one or both of the parties is very young or has severe emotional and addictive disorders, there are risk factors to weigh seriously before marriage. The Church provides sound direction along these lines in stressing that the covenant of marriage can be made only by adults who are mentally, emotionally, and spiritually mature. This is because marriage requires us to give of ourselves. A person who has not journeyed sufficiently on the road to generosity and maturity is not capable of a true marriage, no matter what other accomplishments he or she may have already achieved.

Notes

Afterword

Now that we are at the end of our guide, there remains one question that calls for reexploring. It is the most fundamental question associated with the problem of our parents' divorce, and one you will likely ask yourself time and time again: Why embrace the hurt?

Hurt, suffering, grief. Everyone experiences it. None of us want it. Some of us become victims to it. Others try to do everything they can to run away from it. Many of us don't believe it has any value, especially when we are in the throes of pain.

But Jesus showed us otherwise. His passion, death, and resurrection proved that suffering has redemptive value. God took Jesus' suffering and transformed it into something precious and powerful. The same holds true for our suffering, if we enter into it and offer it repeatedly to God, reaching out in the trust that God will strengthen and guide us through it.

Why embrace the hurt? Consider what happens when we don't. We deny, rationalize, and fill our lives with distractions. We cling to whatever will provide an escape. While we may be successful in warding off the intensity of our pain, a nagging emptiness always comes back to haunt us. We may be well aware of all we have to be grateful for and still find ourselves dissatisfied and unfulfilled. It is as if something important is missing in our lives without being able to put a finger on what it is. Grief continues to tap us on the shoulder, demanding attention, taking on new forms, and presenting us with more problems as we ignore it. Our protective mechanisms might give the impression that we're "well adjusted," however they have likely caused injury to our relationships and our self image in the process.

Why embrace the hurt? Because it is the far better price to pay, the only one that doesn't kill our spirit but which ultimately rewards us. Looking back, while my journey of healing was a long and difficult one, I am a better person for having experienced its grief and sorrow. This cross also enabled me to discover God's hopes for me, a way that was not my way, but the path that gifted my life with a deeper purpose.

Why embrace the hurt? Because it is how we show allegiance to God's goodness and unconditional love, an allegiance in which we take and give ourselves a real chance. In exchange for our reaching out when it's scariest and most difficult, God shares with us an extraordinary generosity and transforms our lives into grace, gifting us with a peace and joy far greater than we could have known otherwise.

Resources for Further Growth

Anger

Gottlieb, Miriam M. *The Angry Self: A Comprehensive Approach to Anger Management*. Phoenix, AZ: Zeig, Tucker, and Theisen, Inc., 1999.
Workbook with practical tools and strategies to get better control of anger and create solutions. Also includes relaxation techniques and assignments.

Potter-Efron, Ronald T. *Stop the Anger Now: A Workbook for the Prevention, Containment, and Resolution of Anger*. Oakland, CA: New Harbinger Publications, Inc., 2001.
Workbook of exercises and tips to help prevent, contain, and resolve angry outbursts.

Faith

Gellman, Rabbi Marc and Monsignor Thomas Hartman. *Where Does God Live?* Liguori, MO: Liguori Publications, 1996.
This book takes an ecumenical look at the mysteries surrounding God and answers the simple yet profound questions young people often have about the deity.

Teske, Robert T. and Guideposts Magazine Staff. *The Best Stories from Guideposts: Inspiring Accounts of God's Miraculous Intervention in People's Lives*. Wheaton, IL: Tyndale House Publishers, Inc., 1987.
Inspiring true stories that show how people find hope in times of tragedy and fear by reaching out to God.

Powell, John. *The Challenge of Faith,* Allen, TX: Thomas More Publishing, 1998.
Powell addresses the question of faith, emphasizing that we need an open mind. He also explores how stepping out into faith is the moment of choice that marks an inner awareness of what God is doing in our lives.

Forgiveness

Logue, Judy. *Forgiving the People You Love to Hate.* Liguori, MO: Liguori Publications, 1997.
Using Scripture, personal experience, and psychological insights, this guide helps readers focus on the power of imagination and the freeing of new perspectives that evolve to make forgiveness possible.

Monbourquette, John. *How to Forgive: A Step-by-Step Guide,* Cincinnati, OH: St. Anthony Messenger Press, 2000.
Twelve-step guide which offers practical advice on overcoming the emotional, spiritual, and psychological blocks to true forgiveness. Also includes practical exercises, case histories, anecdotes, and poetry.

Grief

Deits, Bob. *Life After Loss: A Personal Guide Dealing with Death, Divorce, Job Change, and Relocation,* Cambridge, MA: Fisher Books, 1999.
Practical guide with helpful exercises and charts for working through grief. Includes first-hand stories.

Personal Growth

Gustin, Marilyn. *The Courage to Change: Empowering Your Life from the Inside Out.* Liguori, MO: Liguori Publications, 1996.
This book shows how even though we cannot always choose what happens to us, we can choose not to be a victim.

Parent, Remi. *Life to the Limits: From Everyday Losses to New Possibilities.* Liguori, MO: Liguori Publications, 1998.
For those who are discouraged or disillusioned, this book helps bring meaning to losses and limitations.

Powell, John, *Why Am I Afraid to Tell You Who I Am?* Allen, TX: Thomas More Publishing, 1993.
Insights on growing in self-awareness, communication skills, and interpersonal relationships. Addresses working with emotions and moving beyond ego-defense methods so honest self-communication and identity can be realized.

Valles, Carlos G. *I Love You, I Hate You: The Double-Edged Nature of Human Relationships*, Liguori, MO: Liguori Publications, 1992.
This book casts a revealing light on the conflicting emotions in all relationships.

Prayer

Braybrooke, Marcus. *Learn to Pray: A Practical Guide to Faith and Inspiration*, San Francisco, CA: Chronicle Books, 2001.
Illustrated, inspirational guide with over twenty-five step-by-step prayer exercises. Includes prayers and wisdom from contemporary and historical sources, including Saint Francis of Assisi, Mahatma Gandhi, and the prophet Muhammad.

Hanegraff, Hank. *The Prayer of Jesus: Secrets to Real Intimacy with God*, Nashville, TN: Word Publishing Group, 2001.
Concise, practical guide that reveals Jesus' teaching and modeling on the essentials of prayer.

Wilkinson, Bruce H. *The Prayer of Jabez for Teens*, Sisters, OR: Multnomah Publishers, Inc., 2001.
Includes peer-based stories, supporting scriptures and interactive questions regarding how to pray the prayer of Jabez.

Relationships

Perrotta, Kevin and Gregory K. Popcak. *God Help Me! These People Are Driving Me Nuts: Making Peace With Difficult People*, Chicago, IL: Loyola Press, 2001.
Practical, humorous book that integrates psychology, case studies, and healing principles. Includes insights into Christian love and strategies for coping with people who won't change their self-destructive ways.

About the Author

Lynn Cassella is the founder of Faith Journeys Foundation, Inc., an organization dedicated to supporting children of divorce in their journey toward growth. Through retreats and discussion groups, Lynn invites young people to share their dilemmas while guiding them with a positive, challenging, God-centered view that has worked for her. She speaks from over thirty years personal experience, a sincere love for young people, and a foundation in Catholic teaching. Lynn is available to speak at conferences and retreats on subjects such as forgiveness, faith, and understanding the effects of separation and divorce on children (www.faithjourneys.org).

She and her husband, George, live in Baltimore, MD.